DITCH *the* DEBT *and* GET RICH

BY EFFIE ZAHOS

Published in 2021 by Are Media Books, Australia.
Are Media Books is a division of Are Media Pty Ltd.

ARE MEDIA

Chief executive officer Brendon Hill

ARE MEDIA BOOKS

General manager: Publishing Sally Eagle

Author Effie Zahos

Editor Maria Bekiaris

Researcher Nicola Field

Sub-editors Bob Christensen, Debbie Duncan

Managing editor Stephanie Kistner

Art director & designer Jeannel Cunanan

Operations manager David Scotto

Cover photographer Alana Landsberry

Cover stylist Alex Wilson

Cover hair stylist David Connelly

Cover make-up artist Eloise Proust

Printed in China
by 1010 Printing International

A catalogue record for this book is available
from the National Library of Australia.
ISBN 978-1-92586-558-5
© Are Media Pty Limited 2021
ABN 18 053 273 546
This publication is copyright.
No part of it may be reproduced or
transmitted in any form without
the written permission of the publisher.

Published by Are Media Books,
a division of Are Media Pty Ltd,
54 Park St, Sydney; GPO Box 4088,
Sydney, NSW 2001, Australia
Ph +61 2 8116 9334
www.aremediabooks.com.au

ORDER BOOKS

phone 1300 322 007 (within Australia)
or order online at
www.aremediabooks.com.au

DISCLAIMER

While I hope this book helps you on your path to financial success I'd hate for you
to solely rely on it. It was never written as a substitute for, nor was it intended to replace or
supersede, independent or other professional advice.
I am not a financial advisor so the information in this book is intended as general guidance only.
Great information, though, and there's plenty to be said about being financially savvy.
Given that the circumstances and investment objectives of individual readers have not been taken
into account in the preparation of material in this book, please be sure to make your own inquiries
before making any investment decisions.
This edition includes information current at the time of writing.

Dedication

To my lifelong bestie, Angela. This book is for you.
Your enthusiasm for saving and making money is
inspiring. While I enjoy getting your random money
questions via text, the good news is that all the
answers, my friend, are now in here . . .
I know you can do it! And no, you won't have
to buy the book – this one is on me!

Contents

DITCH *the* DEBT *and* GET RICH

I'm not very good at remembering names (for the record, I am working on this) but I do remember Debbie's. She was the very first person to whom I ever gave a financial makeover.

In 1998, Debbie wrote to Channel 9's *Money* show, where I was working as a researcher, to ask for help turning her finances around.

As a single mum with a dependant, and unexpected bills to pay, Debbie had fallen behind and found herself in serious debt. As well as her home loan she had four other personal loans.

It took some convincing, but we managed to get Debbie's lender to let her consolidate those personal debts into her home loan. (This option wasn't as mainstream as it is now.) Debbie then diverted some of the savings into her home loan.

I have often wondered how things worked out for Debbie, and oddly enough, she reached out to me recently to say that she is doing just fine – no debt!

Preface

I'd like to think that I've helped plenty more 'Debbies' since then and will continue to do so. I'm just as excited about helping people now as I was when I first took on that role as a researcher 22 odd years ago.

That is why I have written this book – to help as many people as I can.

So, what do I mean by ditching the debt and getting rich? It's not necessarily about having a ridiculous amount of wealth. It's all about enjoying a stress-free financial life.

.It means that you can stop living from pay to pay. You can get rid of your debt. You can buy a home. You can start investing. You can build your perfect portfolio. You can retire on $50,000 a year.

Yes, there are a lot of 'cans' in this book. That's because when it comes to money just about all of us can do it ... that is, ditch the debt and get rich.

At the end of the day, someone is probably always going to be earning more than you or be richer than you, and that's fine. You just want to be in the best financial position possible and that's what this book is all about.

It all starts with mastering your money mindset and understanding why you do what you do. As the great Warren Buffett once said: "If you can't control your emotions, you can't control your money."

I'll be there to guide you each step of the way, with practical tips, facts, figures and strategies. Of course, seek independent advice when needed.

I hope this book is the nudge you need to stop just getting by and start thriving. You can do it!

Why you should never save your credit card details online (the answer has nothing to do with security), and why FOJI (fear of joining in) is just as bad as FOMO (fear of missing out) when it comes to investing. This section is all about recognising your money personality (there's a reason why you do what you do) and how this can help you improve your financial situation. Plus, the mind games to watch out for so you don't part with your hard-earned dollars too easily.

PART I

MASTER YOUR MONEY MINDSET

—

I CAN...

Get to know my money personality

I've always been fascinated by why we do what we do. Why is it that some of us are always the first to buy a round of drinks on a Friday night while others are happy to accept a first round but then quietly walk away when it's their turn to shout?

Why is it that some of us on, say, $60,000 a year are better with our cash than those on $160,000 a year?

Why is it that some of us have no fear when it comes to investing yet others just keep saying, "I'm gonna do it!"

Knowing what drives your financial decisions is the first step towards reaching your money goals, which is why I thought it was important to kickstart this book by looking at how you can get to know your money personality. Understanding why you do what you do is one of the first steps to helping you shape your approach to spending, saving, and investing.

When it comes to money, the 'why we do it' is more complicated than the 'how we do it', which is why I caught up once again with renowned behavioural economist Phil Slade, author of *Going Ape S#!t!*, who says our money personality is not genetic like the colour of our eyes or skin tone. Rather, our money mindset is learnt, and it's a reflection of how we have worked out how to survive and navigate the world around us. Phil's insight into why we do what we do was invaluable for my section on how you can master your money mindset.

A study from the UK's Cambridge University found that our core behaviours and money habits can be formed by age seven. By the time we hit puberty, the lessons we've learnt around money are pretty hard-baked into our instinctive reactivity. So, naturally, changing our money personality can be a slow process. But it can be done. Your money personality isn't set in stone – you can master your money mindset.

Phil says our financial attitudes and monetary behaviours are like windows into our soul, into the very essence of who we are and how we think.

When we fail to understand ourselves, we create all sorts of cognitive blind spots and bad money habits that undermine our ability to build sustainable wealth. Knowing your money personality is to light the pathway to financial success.

Know your money mindset

If you aren't convinced about how our money personality can make – or break – our ability to get ahead financially, let me introduce you to two women. Both are well educated, both have professional jobs and earn decent incomes. Oh, and both are real people about my age (don't ask!); I've just changed their names.

Laura is careful with her money. She has significant cash savings, owns her home and has near-zero personal debt. She is also a self-confessed 'real estate junkie'. Laura regularly trawls online listings looking for an investment property. She's been doing it for years, but has never actually taken the plunge and put her money down.

As Laura recently lamented to me, "If I'd purchased around 10 years ago, I'd have almost paid a place off." The trouble is, she just can't bring herself to part with her brass.

Now let's meet Zoe. She has one of the most impressive shoe collections I've ever seen. I'm talking cupboards full of shoes – still in their boxes, many never worn. She also has a pretty good wardrobe of clothing but the shoes are the real show-stopper. In fact, Zoe has spent so much on her shoe collection that she has a solid credit card debt and virtually no cash savings.

Maybe you recognise a bit of yourself in Laura or Zoe. The main point is that it's their money mindset, not their income, that is holding both women back financially. So, let's look at the main money personalities to see if you can pick which categories Laura, Zoe, or you, fall into.

5 main money personalities

There are five dominant money personalities – spender, saver, debtor, investor and avoider. Of course, these five money personalities have many different shades. You could be a social value spender – you buy things to boost your self-esteem. Or you may spend up big so others can admire you.

Whatever your shade, the end result is that if someone is selling, you're buying. The important point here is to be proactive and take the time to understand your money type. Some behavioural economists say people's attitude to money can mimic certain animals (I've taken the liberty to add in some of my own animals).

So, let's have some fun, and take a trip into the wild to see which furry (or feathered) critter best describes your money mindset.

1. PEACOCK – THE SPENDER

If you've ever seen a peacock fan its tail, you've almost certainly had a 'wow!' response. It's so impressive but, of course, it's all done for show to attract a mate. A peacock's gorgeous tail can act as a drag in flight.

It's much the same with human Peacocks. They show off their money, often lavishing gifts on friends and wearing the latest styles to impress everyone. But all that spending can come at the cost of an empty bank account or a super-sized credit card debt. Of course there are various levels of spenders and status spending is just one type of spending.

Tips to break the cycle

If you love spending, you could be a Peacock. But ask yourself, who is benefiting from it all? Retailers, yes. But probably not you. To break the spending cycle, try the 'sleep-on-it' test. If you're tempted to buy an item, walk away and sleep on it. Think about why you're really making the purchase. Is it all part of keeping up with the Joneses? Have you just received a pay bonus? What is the trigger? Go back and have another look at the item. Chances are it won't seem so exciting the second time around.

2. SQUIRREL – THE SAVER

Squirrels are cute and fluffy, and crazy about hoarding nuts. If you're a super saver, you could be a Squirrel. Having some cash behind you makes sense; the trouble is that Squirrels can take it to extremes. They can be so risk averse that they don't invest any of those savings or do anything to help their money grow.

Tips to break the cycle

Saving is not the same as investing, and if you relate to the Squirrel, a simple way to break through the fear barrier is by taking baby steps. Start out small, leaving the bulk of your cash intact. As your comfort levels and confidence grow, you'll realise that investing doesn't mean handing over control of your money – it's about getting more from it.

3. SLOTH – THE DEBTOR

Besides being super cute, sloths are known to be slow, but it's not out of laziness. In fact, it's a survival mechanism. Sloths creep along to avoid being seen by predators that look for signs of movement.

50%
OF PEOPLE ATE, DRANK AND SMOKED MORE DUE TO THEIR FINANCIAL SITUATION, ACCORDING TO THE FINANCIAL MINDFULNESS FSI REPORT, SEPTEMBER 2020.

When it comes to money, human Sloths move slowly, too, but typically because they're weighed down with debt, living payday to payday, and regularly maxing out their credit card. That'll slow anyone down!

Tips to break the cycle

Sloths like to spend but unlike Peacocks they're not worried about status. They simply don't put much effort into keeping their financial assets in order. Some creative thinking can get money Sloths moving again. If this sounds like your money personality, use an app to keep track of your daily expenses, check your bank account more often and don't allow yourself to borrow too much from friends or fast-money outlets. Set up a regular transfer of funds out of your everyday account and into your credit card or loan account.

4. OWL – THE INVESTOR

Fun fact: Owls can rotate their necks 270 degrees, letting them carefully inspect everything. If you get a hoot out of regularly checking your portfolio, you could be an Owl. You're a pretty good money manager, you'd jump institutions for a 0.5% increase in your savings rate, and you swoop in to pick up hot investment opportunities.

Tips to break the cycle

Who needs to break this sort of cycle? If you fit this picture, give yourself a pat on the back. Just remember to keep the emotion out of investing. If anxiety sees you constantly trading, your investments could end up underperforming.

5. OSTRICH – THE AVOIDER

The Ostrich is someone who would rather bury their head in the sand than organise their finances. They fail to make long-term investment decisions and leave everything to luck or fate. Out of sight, out of mind! The trouble is that by continually avoiding the real issues around taking care of their money, Ostriches can never be at their financial best.

Tips to break the cycle

If the Ostrich sounds like you, it's important to have an action plan. Create a simple list with no more than two goals. Set dates to achieve them, have milestones to tick off, and share your goals with a money buddy to help you stay motivated and accountable to your plan.

5 MAIN MONEY PERSONALITIES

There are essentially five dominant money personalities and people's attitude to money can mimic certain animals. Which furry (or feathered) critter best describes you?

PEACOCK
THE
SPENDER

Does this sound like you?

- Money is meant to be spent!
- I deserve this!

SQUIRREL
THE
SAVER

Does this sound like you?

- I save regularly
- I prefer having my money in cash

SLOTH
THE
DEBTOR

Does this sound like you?

- I don't follow a budget
- I use credit to supplement my income

OWL
THE
INVESTOR

Does this sound like you?

- I check my investments every day
- I would move accounts for just a 0.5% difference

OSTRICH
THE AVOIDER

Does this sound like you?

- I always say: "I'm gonna do it!"
- I've never looked at my super statement

Get to know your money personality

Maybe you recognise yourself in one of these five personalities.
As for the two women I mentioned earlier, I'm pretty sure that Laura
is a Squirrel and Zoe definitely fits the bill for a Peacock.

What's more likely is that you're a combination of different money
personalities. Human beings are complex, and as Phil notes, our
money personality is less about boxes or categories and more
about spectrums.

Not only can you have a mix of different money personalities but you can
also change over time as you learn to keep the negative and more reactive
aspects of these money personalities in check.

Having said that though, Phil suggests focusing on your dominant type
and creating some simple rules of thumb around that. What matters is
that you start thinking about your money personality.

Your money mind can impact relationships

Your money mindset isn't just about you. It can also impact your
relationships. When a Squirrel and Peacock get together, it's a fair bet
that at some point feathers and fur will start flying. So, it's worth having
a money conversation with your partner about which money personality
you each identify with.

If your money personalities clash, don't focus on the behaviour. Phil says
it's important to take a deeper look at the problems that the behaviour
is trying to solve, which can have very little to do with a bank balance.
A spender might be splashing cash to make themselves feel good. A saver
might be refusing to take risks because they want to be seen as a good
provider.

"If all you do is accost someone about their behaviour without addressing
the root cause, it could make the problem worse. If you help address their
problem in another way, then the maladaptive money behaviours often
simply vanish over time," Phil explains.

Make the most of your money mind

It's not always easy being honest with ourselves, especially when it comes to admitting our shortcomings. But not understanding your money personality is like having a mischievous child whose behaviour you turn a blind eye to. Ignoring that behaviour may lead them to create all sorts of mayhem and mischief. Now imagine handing your life savings to that kid, and expecting them to take sensible steps with the cash. Things will end badly. Yet in a sense, this is exactly what we are doing when we ignore our money personality.

There's a little bit of that mischievous kid inside each of us and Phil argues that understanding our money personality is like opening our eyes to that wayward inner child, and helping them learn, mature and behave in more appropriate ways.

No matter which of the five money personalities you relate to, it is important to recognise your weak spots. Phil points out that getting a better idea of your money mindset is like drawing a map to avoid potholes in the road ahead.

Once you know where the hazards are, you can maximise opportunities by focusing on a clearer path. This brings confidence and clarity, and helps you get the most out of life – and more from your money.

FAST FACT

CHANGING YOUR SELF-TALK CAN HELP TURN YOUR MINDSET AROUND. FOR EXAMPLE, STOP SAYING: "I CAN'T AFFORD THAT!" AND START SAYING: "I CHOOSE NOT TO BUY THAT." YOU'RE LESS LIKELY TO FEEL AS IF YOU'RE MISSING OUT ON SOMETHING AND MORE LIKELY TO FEEL IN CONTROL BECAUSE YOU'RE MAKING A FIRM DECISION.

ACTION PLAN

☐ Take the time to get to know your money type.

☐ You can have a mix of different money personalities, but you can also change over time as you master the negative aspects of a certain trait.

☐ When you know your traits, you'll be less reactive and more responsive.

☐ Take the steps to manage your bad traits.

☐ There is no right or wrong trait, just understand the triggers and put fixes in place.

☐ When money personality clashes happen, don't focus on the behaviour. Instead focus on the problem the behaviour is trying to solve.

I CAN...

Stop being a wine snob

I love my wine. Pinot grigio is my go-to summer pick – a delicate light-bodied white. On cold winter nights I prefer shiraz – a bold and ballsy flavour.

I may sound like a wine snob but I'm not. For one thing I don't swirl my tipple of choice before I drink it. The other thing that gives away the fact that I know nothing about wine is that I often buy my wine based on the price of a bottle. Don't judge me but, for whatever reason, I think the more expensive a bottle is, the better it must taste.

Unfortunately, I know I've fallen for the oldest trick in the marketing book – prestige pricing. While this sounds absolutely absurd, I'm not alone. Prestige pricing often works on pricier products like cars but can work just as well on less expensive items like wine.

Phil Slade, behavioural economist and author of *Going Ape S#!t!* says there are a few psychological drivers that fuel this perception.

One is a simple trick called 'anchoring'. I have a little more to say on this later but as Phil points out: "We simply don't know the actual value of most things, so by making it more expensive it implicitly signals that it must be more valuable."

Another key driver evolves from scarcity. "When something is more expensive it makes it feel scarcer, and scarcity drives demand," says Phil.

Of course, we can justify just about any purchasing decision and it seems the more irrational it is, the greater the justification.

Phil offers the example of two cars mechanically identical. One carries a prestige badge while the other doesn't.

Paying double for the badge gives some consumers an instant status lift. However, after the purchase, consumers will often consider all the ways the more expensive purchase will last longer, be less likely to break down and so on – essentially feeling compelled to make all sorts of judgements about the brand to justify the spend.

"Our brains have to think more expensive is better or we have to admit we've been taken for a ride ... literally," says Phil.

As for my problem with buying wine based on price, Phil says it's one of the best examples of being irrational. Lucky me!

As he says, the price of the wine or the number of medals on it rarely correlates with the quality. But give someone an average wine and then tell them it costs $150 per bottle and see how their estimation of the wine improves! Nothing to do with the quality of the wine, just a higher price that fundamentally shifts value perception. We think: "It must be good if someone was prepared to pay $X for it!"

With that in mind, let's take a look at some of the marketing traps deployed to take our hard-earned dollars and how we can be smarter when it comes to parting with our cash.

The mind games

1. ONE-CLICK ORDERING

The act of placing an item in your online shopping cart, without any intention of buying, can give you the same rush and excitement as hitting the stores.

For whatever reason, plenty of us like to treat online shopping carts as window shopping. The trouble is that retailers know this, which is why there's one-click ordering.

One-click ordering streamlines the shopping process. You pick a default set of shipping and billing options and from then on all you need to do is click on a single button and everything that's in your cart comes to your front door.

It's extremely easy, convenient and fast. So fast that you don't have time to consider whether or not what you have in your basket is what you really want.

Tip: Avoid setting up a one-click ordering process, especially if you're an impulse buyer.

2. FEAR-BASED MARKETING

'Only 1 left!' 'Limited time only.' '20% off until midnight only!' Retailers know that they can scare you into buying products, which is why you'll often see these messages to nudge you along.

It creates a certain sense of urgency, which pushes us to buy out of fear that we might miss out on something.

Of course, fear-based marketing doesn't have to be negative either. Think of clubs where you need to pay membership fees in order to get further discounts. Costco does this well. By limiting access to members only, the message here is that you may miss out on exclusive deals if you don't sign up.

Tip: Understand that scarcity drives demand. Walk away, take a deep breath and ask yourself, do you really need it or is scarcity making you want it?

3. DECOY PRICING

Have you ever bought a more expensive item because the price of another influenced you? If so, you've probably experienced the decoy effect, or as Phil calls it, the 'anchoring' effect. This is a pricing method designed to 'force' customer choice.

National Geographic ran an experiment to test how the decoy effect influenced customers to buy a large popcorn over a small or medium one.

First, they offered one group of moviegoers two choices – a small bucket of popcorn for $3 and a large bucket at $7. Nearly everyone went for the small. It appears the $7 bucket just felt like a rip-off.

The next group was offered three choices – a small bucket for $3, a medium bucket (the decoy) for $6.5 and a large one for $7.

MARKETING MIND GAMES

There are a number of psychological tactics used by retailers to make us buy more. Here are a few to watch out for.

REMOVE THE COMMA

Researchers have found removing commas can make the price seem lower.

'RULE OF 100'

Percentage discounts are used on small values to make it look like a better deal.

ESSENTIALS AT THE BACK

Milk and eggs are at the back of supermarkets so you're tempted to buy other items along the way.

PAYMENTS IN INSTALMENTS

People are anchored on the lower price. It's why 'buy now, pay later' is so successful.

SEPARATE SHIPPING

$28
+ FREE SHIPPING

$24
+ $4 SHIPPING

By separating the shipping price people focus on the base price.

PAYING UPFRONT

A fixed price upfront removes the pain of uncertainty and paying later. Think Uber.

All they did was add a medium bucket and then suddenly the large one became irresistible. Everyone was buying the large bucket because when they compared it to the medium offer it represented better value.

In the end, though, they all spent more. That's the end goal with decoy pricing – to get you to spend more.

Tip: Only buy what you need and don't be swayed by what you perceive to be better value.

4. FREE TRIALS

How many streaming services do you now subscribe to, thanks to a very simple but clever marketing trick – free trials. Free trials work well because often we are unwilling to try something new, especially if we have to pay for it. Take away the pain of paying and chances are we'll be more inclined to take up the free trial.

The trouble is a free trial is just that – free for only a limited time. Once we've tried it, we are pretty much hooked and then if we have to give it up, it can conjure up feelings of loss.

Tip: Remember that free trials are only for a limited time. Make a diary note to 'unsubscribe'. If you just can't let a particular subscription go, ditch another one of your existing subscriptions instead to save money.

5. FREE GIFTS/CASHBACKS

Cosmetic companies have this trick down pat. Spend $100 and you'll get a free make-up bag with miniature creams and lipsticks. The lipstick might not be a colour you'd usually wear but, hey, that didn't stop you from spending $100.

Banks also try the old cashback deal … well, what's not to like about getting money back after you make a purchase?

The retailer loves it because they don't have to discount the product thereby undervaluing the proposition, and you love it because you get cash back or a free gift. It's a win-win situation … but is it?

Let's take a look at an example. You get $2000 cash back by simply taking out a home loan with one particular lender. Let's assume the rate on the loan is 2.59%. At the time of writing this represented a competitive interest rate as the average variable rate was 3.47%, according to comparison site Canstar.

Do you:

A) Take the money and run; this lender deserves your business.

B) Take the money but put it back on your mortgage.

C) Forgo the cash and take out a loan with the cheaper interest rate.

I asked Canstar to crunch the numbers for each of these scenarios and the results may surprise you.

If you go with option A it will cost you a massive $7,701 in interest at the end of five years when compared to the cheapest standard variable rate on the market.

Go for B and things are a fraction better but you'll still pay $7,430 more in interest over five years. So, C is the clear winner here.

Of course, there are a lot of assumptions here: one is that you can in fact get the cheapest rate on the market; and the second is that interest rates will remain the same for the next five years.

Tip: When confronted with 'free steak knives' put the knives back in the drawer and ask yourself if you would buy the product on its own merits.

FAST FACT

PHIL SLADE SAYS YOU NEED TO GO TO THE SHOPS WITH AN OPEN MIND. IF YOU GO IN SAYING, "I AM GOING TO BUY STEAK", THEN YOU'RE MORE LIKELY TO PURCHASE THE 'LAST STEAK' IN THE SHOP IRRESPECTIVE OF HOW EXPENSIVE IT IS. HOWEVER, IF YOU'RE OPEN TO ALTERNATIVES, YOU MIGHT BUY A DIFFERENT CUT OF MEAT THAT IS ON SALE (WHATEVER IT IS). THEN YOU'RE LESS LIKELY TO GET CAUGHT UP IN A PANIC BUY.

ACTION PLAN

- ☐ *Know what you want.*
- ☐ *Be flexible with what you buy.*
- ☐ *Buy only what you need.*
- ☐ *Understand the marketing ploys at play.*
- ☐ *Put in measures so your decisions aren't swayed.*
- ☐ *Being a brand snob costs you.*

I CAN...

Control my fear of investing

For me, the fear of losing $50 is far greater than the joy of winning $50. It probably explains why I don't gamble. Why am I so afraid of losing money? Well, it all comes down to what behavioural economists call loss aversion – that is, when 'losses loom larger than gains'. It's also the reason why most of us tend to remember price increases rather than price decreases.

Phil Slade, behavioural economist and author of *Going Ape S#*t!* says our fear of losing stems from our survival mechanism. "When coming across an empty cave, those who fear what might be inside are more likely to survive than those who don't. Natural selection favours those who are risk averse, and so taking $50 away from you hurts to a greater degree than the joy you receive by being given $50."

While loss aversion is a natural human behaviour that exists to protect us, it can sometimes do the opposite. It may end up influencing our decisions so that we miss out on potential gains.

Let's say, for example, that you're afraid to invest in the sharemarket because you are worried about losing all your money. In this case, fear of joining in (FOJI) can be just as bad as fear of missing out (FOMO).

FOJI is an anxiety that may prevent you from moving your cash from a safe bank account to, say, the sharemarket. You know that cash in the bank won't make you rich and that over the long term shares could, but because of FOJI you stay put.

One way to try to overcome this fear is to flip your thinking around. Think about it this way: If you don't invest you run the risk of not having enough money for a comfortable retirement.

Another way to take control of your fear is to get an understanding of how investing works. Sure, the sharemarket may go up and down but if you drip-feed your money into your investment you may be somewhat protected, thanks to dollar cost averaging. Dollar cost averaging is when you invest regularly over a long period of time. This allows you to buy more when prices are low and less when prices are high. The end result? You get a better average price. This knowledge in itself may help you curb your FOJI.

Of course, one thing you don't want to do is to go too far and end up going on an investment bender because you're worried you may miss out. FOMO is an emotional reaction that drives you to invest because you feel that if you don't you will miss out on an opportunity of a lifetime. It isn't a good money-making strategy.

Let me give you an example. Afterpay was trading at just $8.90 on 23 March 2020, but by 31 August 2020 its share price was $91.44. That's a 927% jump in price in a little less than six months.

96

THE NUMBER OF POSITIVE YEARS THE AUSTRALIAN SHAREMARKET HAS HAD OVER A 119-YEAR PERIOD (1900-2017).

How does this make you feel? Like you're missing out? Like you need to jump in and buy this stock? If yes, then that's FOMO talking.

Or would you have stayed calm, done some research and assessed the risks and opportunities of that company? If so, then that's the investor in you talking. (For more tips, see Chapter 12: I can pick my own shares.) One of Warren Buffett's most famous investment sayings sums this up perfectly: "Be fearful when others are greedy. Be greedy when others are fearful."

Interestingly, Phil says research shows that it's not experience in the sharemarket that makes us better investors, but how well we deal with the pain of loss when things don't go to plan and what we do to recoup losses. "The more pain we feel in the loss, the more likely we are to make risky investments to make up for the pain. The less pain felt, the less we are driven to alleviate that pain," he explains.

There is no stronger emotional driver that influences our behaviour more than fear.

5 common financial fears and how to deal with them

1. I COULD LOSE IT ALL!

Yes, you could. But then again cash left in a bank account also could lose you money. That's because although right now inflation may be low, interest rates are even lower. The wash-up is that you're not being compensated for the loss of money's purchasing power.

The fact is that while markets fluctuate – and that includes both sharemarket and property market – discipline, time and patience can pay off. Vanguard's 2020 index chart shows that, since 1990, an initial $10,000 investment in the broad Australian sharemarket would have yielded 8.9%pa and grown to $130,457, while an investment in US shares would have returned 10.3%pa to reach $186,799. A $10,000 investment in cash would have returned 5.1%pa growing to $44,172 over the same period.

Tip: Start small. You can build up your confidence by starting with lower-risk investments such as bonds. Micro-investing apps are also a great way to build up confidence without needing large sums of money. You can then start putting your money into investment opportunities that carry a higher risk for a potentially higher return. (Check out Chapter 15: I can build my perfect portfolio.)

2. IT'S ALL TOO COMPLICATED

"If you want to conquer fear, don't sit at home and think about it. Go out and get busy." – Dale Carnegie, self-improvement guru.

This certainly applies to investing. Each day you procrastinate about investing is another day you may have missed out on an opportunity.

I get it, the investment world is full of buzzwords, acronyms and complicated strategies, but by keeping things simple you should be able to curb those investment fears. Education can also play an important role in helping you manage this fear.

Try to concentrate on what you need and want to reach your goals, the risks involved and, of course, make sure you're not paying too much to do so.

Building wealth is about buying good quality assets and holding them for a reasonable amount of time. If you can ride out the bumps then you should end up doing pretty well.

As for where to invest, don't overcomplicate things. There really are only a handful of options you can invest in – yourself, cash, fixed income, property and equities. There's nothing mysterious about these asset classes and you'll learn more throughout the book.

Tip: Investing can be as complicated as you want it to be. You can do it on your own. Get a money buddy, use a robo-advisor, or see a financial advisor. Just be sure to act and don't be afraid to get expert advice when needed.

3. YOU NEED MONEY TO MAKE MONEY

The old saying that "It takes money to make money" is somewhat true. It certainly makes it easier, but (and this is a big but) you don't need a lot of money to start building wealth.

In fact, you can start investing with as little as $100. I have dedicated a chapter to this very topic – Chapter 11: I can invest with just $100 a week. Thanks to fractional investing, investing has never been easier. Fractional investing is when a platform buys a whole share, for example, and divides it up so that you can invest in a share of a share.

Keep an eye on the fees, though. The smaller your balance, the bigger the impact fees can have.

Tip: For investors starting out, fractional investing is a great way to pick up some financial nous.

4. I DON'T KNOW WHEN TO JUMP IN/JUMP OUT

Nobody really does. Unless you're an active day trader, I wouldn't be too concerned with this one. The phrase 'time in the market is better than timing the market' applies here.

Ironically, often the best course of action is no action. Let me explain ... in a falling market you may be tempted to move your investments out of a balanced option, for example, into a conservative option. If you do this, you crystallise your losses and if you don't get your timing right you could miss out on the rebound when you switch back.

Tip: Work out some solid investment rules and write them down where you can see them easily. For example: "I will invest no more than x% of my total capital in any one stock." "I will take most profit at x% to x%." "For every dollar I spend on renovations I need it to return x%." Phil says knowing that you have an agreed exit plan lowers fear and increases confidence to take hold of potential opportunities.

5. WHAT'S THE POINT – I'LL NEVER HAVE ENOUGH TO RETIRE

Knowledge, preparation and action are the three key ingredients required to get you started in investing. It's not unusual to feel overwhelmed when it comes to building wealth – especially if you're just looking at the end picture.

According to the Association of Superannuation Funds of Australia, to have a 'comfortable' retirement, single people will need $545,000 in retirement savings, and couples will need $640,000. It sounds like a lot – and it is – but break it down to smaller chunks and it may feel more achievable thanks to time and the power of compound interest.

Let's say that you invest $5,000 at an interest rate of 6% a year and you do not add any further contributions. At the end of the 12th year your money would have doubled. Simple as that. It's no wonder Albert Einstein called compound interest the 'eighth wonder of the world'.

Tip: Work backwards and put your current investment strategy to the test. Will it help you reach your goal? If not, then you may need to start investing and not just saving.

Phil's tips for overcoming fear

TALK TO YOURSELF

Ask yourself, "What would X do?" Think of a mentor you have a lot of financial respect for and simply imagine what their response would be. How proud or disappointed would they be if you told them about your plans?

VISUALISE THE WORST

Visualise the worst possible outcome and ask yourself if you could survive in this scenario. Fear is often accompanied by unrealistic projections of how bad something might be. Even in the worst version of the outcome, we are often okay. If you can visualise the worst possible outcome and then the likely possible outcome, you'll end up somewhere between a positive outlook and the fear that is influencing your judgement.

BREATHE

Practise mindful and meditative activities. Lowering your emotional state and calming your mind help you make better and less fear-based decisions. Studies that have looked at traders on high-pressure trading floors have shown that investors who spend five minutes every couple of hours meditating increase profits and are less susceptible to FOMO or being overly reactive when a share loses value (fear of loss).

FAST FACT

INVESTORS MAY TRADE TOO OFTEN BECAUSE OF AN OVERCONFIDENCE BIAS ACCORDING TO A REPORT BY RUSSELL INVESTMENTS. IT FOUND THAT HUMANS TEND TO OVERESTIMATE OR EXAGGERATE THEIR ABILITY TO SUCCESSFULLY PERFORM TASKS. RUSSELL INVESTMENTS' GLOBAL ANALYSIS SHOWED THAT THE AVERAGE INVESTOR'S INCLINATION TO CHASE PAST PERFORMANCE HAS COST THEM 1.8% ANNUALLY IN THE 34-YEAR PERIOD FROM 1984 TO 2017.

ACTION PLAN

- [ ] *Ask yourself what is stopping you from investing.*
- [ ] *Agree on a change and put in strategies to overcome your fears.*
- [ ] *Keep things simple.*
- [ ] *Start small but invest often.*
- [ ] *Visualise the worst.*
- [ ] *Put an exit strategy in place.*
- [ ] *Breathe.*

You know that feeling … the heaviness, the anxiousness of carrying debt. There are no short-term fixes to getting that monkey off your back. In this section, you'll get a blueprint to help you put a strategy in place so you can stop asking, "When is payday?" The rest is up to you. You'll create a bare-bones budget to help you break the cycle of living from pay to pay. You'll also have the facts and figures to help you choose between the snowball or avalanche method of paying off your debts, and you'll get a six-point plan to help you prepare for any curveballs.

PART II

GET THAT MONKEY OFF YOUR BACK

—

I CAN...

Stop living from pay to pay

Chapter four

"Money's too tight to mention. Three more days until payday. I can't wait!"

If that sounds like you then read on. You might be blaming lack of funds. Maybe you feel like you don't earn enough or have too many debts.

The fact is that there may be a very good reason why we are living from pay to pay, but we tend to put the blame on everything and everyone except our own behaviour.

Don't get me wrong – a low income can certainly be one of the main reasons you're short on cash but, in my experience, often income has very little to do with it. A person with a $200,000 salary can have just as much trouble getting by as someone who earns $60,000.

The saying "It's not what you earn that counts but what you spend" is apt here.

With all that in mind, here's your blueprint to help you put a strategy in place so that you can work towards being in a stronger financial position and stop living from pay to pay.

Create a bare-bones budget

If you want to escape the vicious cycle of living from pay to pay, the first thing you need to do is create a bare-bones budget. This is different to a normal budget because it only includes the expenses you need to survive – the ones that mean you'll have a roof over your head, (home-cooked) meals on the table and the lights on – and not the things that would fall under nice-to-have or luxuries. On the next page is a guide to what you should and shouldn't include.

WHAT YOU SHOULD INCLUDE	WHAT YOU SHOULDN'T INCLUDE
• Mortgage repayments/rent • Electricity and gas bills • Groceries • Insurance premiums (car, home and contents, life, income protection) • Minimum debt repayments • Medication • Childcare/school fees • Mobile phone plan • Internet plan • Petrol, public transport • Savings towards an emergency fund	• Dining out/takeaway • Entertainment services such as Netflix or Foxtel • Non-essential clothing • Holidays • Recreational activities/hobbies • Non-essential household items • Personal care such as manicures and cosmetics

Can you cut any of your costs?

When you have all your expenses listed, it's a good idea to go through them individually to see if there are ways to trim the costs.

If you have a mortgage, this is a great place to start as chances are it would be one of your biggest regular expenses. If you can score a cheaper rate, not only will your repayments be lower but you can save big bucks over the life of the loan.

For example, let's assume you have a $500,000 loan and are paying 3.49%pa. By switching to a loan with a lower rate of 2.19%, your repayments would be $334 a month less, saving you $4,008 a year. And you'd pay $100,383 less interest over the life of the loan.

Comparison sites such as Canstar (of which I am Editor-at-Large) can help you track down the best deals. Keep in mind that cheapest doesn't always mean best, so consider the features as well as the price. It's also a good idea to call your existing lender to ask if they can match the rate to save you the hassle of switching.

PAYDAY CIRCLE OF LIFE

Does this sound familiar – you get paid, you feel loaded, you spend up big and then you remember there are bills to pay? This sums up what it feels like to be caught up in the vicious cycle of living pay to pay.

PAYDAY

WAITING WAITING WAITING

NOW I AM
WORRIED

YAY, I'M
LOADED!

DINNER'S
ON ME

BUT I REALLY
NEED THOSE
SHOES! NO
WORRIES – I'LL
MAKE IT WORK!

HANG ON,
I'VE GOT
BILLS TO PAY

NOT SO LOADED
ANYMORE

If your lender doesn't come to the party, refinancing might be the way to go. Just make sure you consider any switching costs and do a break-even analysis to make sure it's worth it. For example, if it will end up costing you $1,000 to switch and you'd save $50 a month in repayments, then it would take you 20 months to 'break even'; but if your repayments were $150 a month lower it would take you about seven months.

If you're renting, you can also look for ways to reduce that expense: is it possible to move to a different location where the rent is cheaper or to a smaller place or share house? It doesn't have to be forever – it can be a temporary solution.

It is also a good time to shop around for better deals on some of your other regular bills such as electricity and gas, mobile and internet plans as well as insurance. You might be surprised by how much you could save on these as well.

To give you an idea, research by Canstar found that the average premium for a home and contents insurance policy is $1,369 but the lowest is $834. So, you could potentially save $535 a year. You could possibly save $573 and $634 on car insurance and hospital insurance respectively.

Do you need to make more money?

Hopefully, you'll find you have enough money coming in to cover the expenses listed in your bare-bones budget but, if not, you may need to explore ways to make more money.

Looking for a new job that pays more is the obvious solution to boost money coming in but that is easier said than done and it may take a while to find something appropriate. While you're waiting to land a new job, look for alternative ways to bring in extra cash.

Sell any unwanted items on Facebook Marketplace, Gumtree or ebay. Or try to get a second casual job in the evenings or on weekends.

Maybe you have a special skill that could help make you a few extra bucks. For example, if you speak a foreign language or play an instrument, could you do some tutoring?

And with the rise of the share economy, there is no shortage of ways to make extra money, whether it's becoming an Uber driver, renting out space in your house, doing odd jobs on Airtasker or pet sitting.

Live on your bare-bones budget temporarily

Even if you feel that you could possibly add in a few nice-to-haves, I would suggest living on your bare-bones budget for a few months – at the very least until you have built up a decent emergency fund.

Having money set aside for a rainy day is vital if you want to stop living pay to pay, which is why I have included it as one of the items in the 'what you should include' list. So, any money 'left over' after meeting all your other necessary expenses should be directed to your emergency fund at this stage. (There is more about creating an emergency fund in Chapter 6: I can deal with curveballs.)

If you have any 'bad' debts such as credit cards or personal loans, ditching those will be your next priority. For tips on how to do this, see Chapter 5: I can get rid of my (bad) debt.

Once you have reached your emergency fund goal, you can revisit your budget and start adding some 'fun' stuff back in, such as the occasional takeaway meal or a Netflix subscription. It's a good idea to reintroduce these little luxuries gradually so that you don't end up struggling to make ends meet again. And make sure you update your budget accordingly.

Before you start adding the indulgences to your budget, I suggest you do two things.

The first is to think long and hard about whether the 'indulgence' is that important to you. Don't put it on your list simply because you have the extra money now. Did you miss those manicures or Friday night Thai takeaway that much while you were living on your bare-bones budget?

The second is to look for ways to not pay more for items than you have to. So, shop around to make sure you are getting the best deal or look for other ways to cut costs.

What does a 'good' budget look like?

A popular budgeting technique is the 70:20:10 plan. This helps you estimate how much of your money you should allocate towards different types of expenses.

This means that you'd divide your monthly take-home pay into:

- 70% for everyday living costs such as rent or home loan, utilities, food, clothing and transport.

- 20% for saving.

- 10% for splurging

You can tweak these percentages. For example, you may find 50:30:20 or 60:30:10 works better for you, but the key is to always have money allocated towards savings.

Tips to help you manage your money

This formula may sound great in theory, but the tough part can be putting it into practice. The good news is that there are a few little tricks to help you better manage your money and stick to your budget.

1. PUT YOUR MONEY INTO BUCKETS

One way to easily manage your money is to break down your expenses into smaller buckets rather than having them all lumped into one. For example, you may have one for school fees, one for groceries, one for bills, one for splurges and so on. How many buckets you have is completely up to you but be sure to name them.

The idea is that when you get paid, you transfer the designated amount into each bucket. This is the modern-day equivalent of the envelope system where you put cash for different expenses into an envelope.

Banks such as Bankwest and Suncorp allow you to create multiple sub-accounts for free or you may opt to open multiple accounts and name them accordingly. Just make sure there are no fees attached to these accounts. For your savings and any other 'buckets' of money that will stay in the account for a longer period, you should also look for an account that is paying a decent rate of interest.

If you have a mortgage and you prefer to have your money in an offset account, this can be trickier. Some institutions offer multiple offset sub-accounts but if yours doesn't, you may opt to keep your savings in the offset account and any money for regular expenses in other accounts.

2. PLAN FOR YOUR IRREGULAR EXPENSES

One way that people often get caught out is not setting aside enough money to cover bills that aren't fortnightly or monthly but rather quarterly, such as electricity and gas, or annually, such as car registration and rates. So that you don't find yourself scrambling for cash to pay these bills, you could use something called 'bill-smoothing'. This involves estimating what that big expense will be and then breaking it down into fortnightly or monthly amounts. For example, if you think your electricity bill will be $1,500 for the year then you put away $125 a month or $58 a fortnight to make sure you have enough when the bill arrives.

You can pay this straight towards your bill, but my suggestion would be to put that money into a savings account so that at least you'll be earning some interest. When you are estimating your big bills, it can be a good idea to add 5% to 10% just in case.

Some service providers – mainly electricity and gas companies – offer formal bill-smoothing arrangements. They estimate your yearly energy costs and tell you how much you need to pay each month. If your actual usage is different from what the provider estimated, they may change your payment amount. If you want to use this option, check that there are no fees involved and find out exactly how it works. It's also worth noting that this means you won't be earning interest.

3. DON'T SPEND MONEY YOU DON'T HAVE

It might sound obvious but given that there are 14,088,998 credit card accounts in Australia in 2020 and buy now, pay later schemes such as Afterpay are growing in popularity, not spending money we don't have appears to be easier said than done for many.

So, keep your credit card at home, cancel any buy now, pay later arrangements, and use cash to pay for things whenever possible.

4. KEEP TRACK OF YOUR SPENDING

It's important to stay on top of your spending so bad habits don't creep in again. This could be as simple as regularly taking a look at your accounts online but there are also helpful apps that track your spending.

A number of apps will let you link your bank accounts or credit cards to give you an overview of your spending all in the one place. They may even automatically put your spending into certain categories, making it easier for you to see where your money is going.

Some apps worth a look include MoneyBrilliant, Pocketbook, Spendee and Frollo.

5. SET FINANCIAL GOALS

Having a list of goals that you want to achieve can be a great motivator. Whether you are working towards saving for a holiday or a house deposit, it might be the extra incentive you need to stick to your budget and stash money into your savings account each payday rather than spending it on things you don't need.

FAST FACT

MORE THAN ONE-QUARTER (26%) OF AUSTRALIANS FEEL THEY ARE NOT LIVING WITHIN THEIR MEANS – THEY SPEND MORE THAN THEY EARN, DON'T SAVE REGULARLY AND DON'T LIMIT THEIR DEBTS, ACCORDING TO CANSTAR'S 2019 CONSUMER PULSE REPORT.

ACTION PLAN

☐ *Put together a bare-bones budget that only includes necessities such as food, shelter, utilities and transport.*

☐ *Go through all your expenses to look for ways to cut costs.*

☐ *Look for ways to boost cash coming in by selling things, finding a higher-paying job or starting a side hustle.*

☐ *Start building an emergency fund. Be sure to automate your savings and have a set amount deposited directly into your emergency fund.*

☐ *Live on your bare-bones budget until you have built up a savings buffer in the form of an emergency fund.*

☐ *Gradually start adding a few 'nice-to-haves' back into your budget.*

☐ *Keep track of your spending so you don't fall back into your old habits.*

I CAN...

Get rid of my (bad) debt

Chapter five

There's no way to sugarcoat this. If you have debt –
and I'm talking about bad debt – you're living beyond
your means. If you have debt you just can't get rid
of, it needs to be your number one priority. It won't
necessarily be easy, as you may have to change some of
your behaviours, but until you get that pesky monkey
off your back it's very hard to move forward.

Putting aside the reasons why you got into debt in the first
place I want to concentrate on how you can get rid of this
burden once and for all.

I am focusing on 'bad' debts here. You accrue bad debt
when you borrow money to buy things that will probably
lose value fairly quickly and don't generate any income.
Think credit cards, personal loans and 'buy now, pay later'
(BNPL) services.

Your home loan or an investment property loan would fall
into the 'good' debt category because you use those debts
to buy assets that help you build wealth. You still don't
want to be carrying it around forever but clearing any bad
debt should definitely be a priority. Bad debt also tends to
be a more expensive form of debt. Think about it. These
days you could easily get a home loan rate of between 2%
and 3%, but most credit card rates are in double digits,
with some as high as 20%.

Take control of your debt

The first step to taking control of your debt is to stop
spending. Don't use your credit card anymore and stop
using BNPL services. If you don't have the cash to pay for
something then the answer is pretty simple – don't buy it!

Make a list of your debts

If you have only one form of bad debt, this step will be pretty quick. On the other hand, if you have multiple outstanding debts it might take you a little longer. Include credit cards, store cards, outstanding BNPL debts, and personal loans.

Next to each debt make a note of the following: the outstanding balance, the interest rate being charged and the minimum monthly repayment. Add everything up to see how much you owe in total.

Create a budget

Take a good look at your spending to identify where things are going wrong. Have you found yourself in debt because you whack everything you want on your credit card or regularly use BNPL services because you don't want to wait?

Or maybe it's because you're simply struggling to make ends meet and you have to resort to credit to meet your everyday expenses.

Whichever category you fall into, it's important to start working on cutting back your spending. If you fall into the first category and your debt is a result of splurging, this step might be easier for you than if you're someone who is finding it tough just to get by.

Go through all your expenses with a fine-tooth comb and figure out what you can delete or what you may be able to get a better deal on.

As I recommended in Chapter 4: I can stop living from pay to pay, I would suggest trying to live on a bare-bones budget for a while and direct any extra money towards paying down those debts. When you reach your goal, you can start adding in some nice-to-haves.

I know that might sound tough but it will help you clear your debt much quicker. If you don't think you can stick to that then at the very least limit the amount of spending on 'wants' such as a pedicure or takeaway twice in a week so that you still have a decent chunk of cash to put towards paying down debt.

Talk to your lenders

It could also be a good idea to talk to any lenders to see if you can negotiate a better rate on your existing debt. Be upfront and let them know that you are experiencing some financial difficulty and ask what they may be able to do to help you out, such as reducing the rate even if it's for a short period of time.

Start cracking down on that debt

Make paying down your debt your number one priority – even more than saving. There's little point stashing money away in a savings account paying less than 3% when chances are you're paying anywhere from 10% to 20% interest on your debt.

The exception to this rule is if you don't have any money set aside in case of emergencies. If that's the case then I would encourage you to put at least $1,000 aside for any unexpected expenses. That way if something crops up, such as car repairs, you won't have to resort to putting the expense on your credit card.

The same applies if you already have money in savings. Keep some aside in your emergency fund and use the remainder to reduce your debt.

Ask yourself if there is anything you can sell and use the proceeds to put towards your debt. And if money comes your way, for example a tax refund, then put that straight onto your credit card.

When it comes to paying down multiple debts, there are a number of different approaches you can take.

Let's look at the main options.

1. SNOWBALL METHOD

With the snowball method you pay off your debt in order from smallest to largest. So, you only make the minimum repayments on the larger debts and put all your extra cash into the smallest debt. When you pay off the first debt you move onto the second smallest debt until that is paid off. You continue in this way until all debts on your list have been cleared.

There is definitely a psychological benefit to using the snowball method because you'll feel a sense of achievement when you pay off a debt – and this will happen quite quickly if you focus on the smaller debt first.

2. AVALANCHE METHOD

With the avalanche method your priority is to pay off the debt with the highest interest rate first (rather than the smallest) and then move down the list by interest rate until all your debt is cleared. So, you make the minimum repayments on any debts with lower rates and pull all your surplus money towards the debt with the highest rate.

While the snowball and avalanche methods may seem similar from a numbers point of view, chances are the avalanche method will give you the better result.

3. TAKING OUT A BALANCE TRANSFER

Balance transfer offers are commonplace these days. The idea is you get a special rate for a limited period if you transfer your debt from a different institution. The most common offer is 0% for six months but you may be able to get a low rate, or even 0%, for an extended period.

Some of the things to consider:

What does the rate revert to once the introductory period is over? Make sure it's still competitive because if you don't manage to pay it off in the promotional period, you may find yourself in the same boat again.

What is the annual fee? A high fee could eat into any interest savings you make.

Is there a balance transfer fee? Some institutions charge a percentage of the balance and again this could really eat into any savings. If you paid a 2% fee on a $5,000 balance, that adds up to $100. To work out what balance transfer deal might be best for you, consider how large your balance is, how much you can afford to pay off each month and how likely you are to stick to this. If you have a large balance and your repayments will be on the lower end then the revert rate will be especially important.

It's also important to be aware that you might not be able to get a balance transfer through a financial institution you have debt with. So, if you have a credit card with a debt from the CBA, you won't be able to transfer your balance to another card with the CBA.

This can also apply to other brands that may fall under the same umbrella such as Westpac and its subsidiaries St.George, Bank of Melbourne and BankSA.

56%

OF 'BUY NOW, PAY LATER' USERS ARE AGED BETWEEN 14-34, ACCORDING TO ROY MORGAN RESEARCH, SEPTEMBER 2019.

Balance transfer limits may apply, which means the new lender may only allow you to transfer a portion of the total limit of the new card. So, if you are approved for a card with a $5,000 limit but the provider has a cap of 80% on balance transfers, it means you can only transfer up to $4,000 of your existing debt onto the card. If your debt is higher than that you'll end up with several debts again, which isn't ideal.

4. CONSOLIDATING YOUR DEBT INTO A PERSONAL LOAN

Another option worth looking into is consolidating all your outstanding debts into a personal loan. The advantage of a personal loan is that you only have to worry about making a single repayment each month, you are forced to make repayments each month, and at the end of the loan term the debt will be gone.

If you take this option, make sure you look for a personal loan with a competitive rate and fees. I'd suggest taking out the loan for the shortest term you can afford the repayments on. Or if you want a buffer take out a loan with a longer term but make higher repayments to clear it faster.

5. CONSOLIDATING IT INTO YOUR HOME LOAN

You could look into consolidating all your debt into your mortgage. You will need to have enough equity in your home, though, to be able to do this.

The risk of this approach is that if you stick to just making the minimum home loan repayments, you are essentially extending your loan and will pay more interest over the long run. If you use your home loan, it's important to make extra repayments to reduce the debt faster.

It's also worth asking if any top-up fees apply and, if so, what they are. If you have a small debt then it might not be worth it.

5 debt-repayment strategies put to the test

So now you know what the main options are, let's take a look at how they stack up. I asked comparison site Canstar to crunch the numbers based on a hypothetical example.

Emma has the following credit card debts and has $350 a month in total to put towards her debts:

1. Balance of $1,500, with a rate of 11.99% and no annual fee.

2. Balance of $3,500, with a rate of 19.99% and a $99 annual fee.

3. Balance of $5,000, with a rate of 13.24% and a $59 annual fee.

As the table on page 55 shows, her best option by far is topping up her home loan. This would end up costing Emma $763 all up.

The next best option is consolidating the debt into a personal loan and she'd end up paying $2,206 in interest and fees. Using the avalanche method would cost her $2,669 – $463 more than the personal loan. The snowball method would set her back $2,975 in interest and fees and the balance transfer is last on the list, costing Emma $3,067.

The results may be different for you depending on the amount of debt you have, the interest you're paying, how much you can afford to repay and so on, but this gives you a rough idea.

DEBT-REPAYMENT STRATEGIES PUT TO THE TEST (TOTAL DEBT OF $10,000)

METHOD	SNOWBALL	AVALANCHE	BALANCE TRANSFER	PERSONAL LOAN	TOP-UP HOME LOAN
	Minimum repayments of 2% or $20 (whichever is greater)	Minimum repayments of 2% or $20 (whichever is greater)	BT rate: 0% for 6 months BT fee: 0% Revert rate: 20.29% Annual fee: $174	Application fee: $210 Interest Rate: 12.38%	Top-up fee: $294 Interest Rate: 3.40%
Total interest paid	$2,501	$2,294	$2,371	$1996	$469
Total fees paid	$474	$375	$696	$210	$294
Total interest & fees	$2,975	$2,669	$3,067	$2,206	$763
Time to repay	3 years	3 years	3 years 2 months	2 years 11 months	2 years 7 months

Source: www.canstar.com.au - 13/08/2020. Assumes three credit card debts totalling $10,000 and repayments of $350 a month. Based on products on Canstar's database. Snowball and Avalanche methods assume median minimum repayments based on personal, unsecured credit cards. Balance Transfer method assumes the average revert rate and annual fee of personal, unsecured credit cards with the most common BT offer used, 0% for 6 months with 0% BT fee. Personal Loan Method assumes the average application fee and interest rate of unsecured 3-year loans available for debt consolidation of $10,000. Home Loan Top-up method assumes the average interest rate and top-up fee of owner occupier, variable loans available for $400,000, 80% LVR and principal and interest repayments; excluding introductory and first home buyer only loans (based on home loans with top up available). All scenarios assume fees are capitalised, with the annual credit card fees applied at the start of each year and the balance transfer, personal loan application and home loan top-up fees applied upfront.

Where to go for help

If it all feels like it's too much and you need some extra help then it's a good idea to talk to a financial counsellor. A good place to start is the National Debt Helpline. You can visit the website ndh.org.au or call them on 1800 007 007.

Life after debt

After you have done all the hard work to ditch your debt, the last thing you want to do is end up back in the same situation. I would get rid of the credit card altogether – or at the very least only keep one with a small limit so that you don't land yourself in trouble – and cancel any BNPL services.

In the past, it was hard to live without a credit card if you wanted to make any online purchases. These days there are plenty of alternatives including debit cards and PayPal.

Here are some other tips to help you stop whacking things on credit:

- Set up your own BNPL account. Put, say, $1,000 in your account and only use this account to shop. When you buy something, pay yourself back in four equal instalments. Chances are when you've saved up the cash and you're staring at it you may not tap into it as much.

- Wait before you buy something. If you see something you want, don't buy it straightaway. Give yourself some breathing space – it might be two days or a week. If you still want it after waiting, go ahead and buy it.

- Calculate how many hours you'll have to work to pay for an item to find out if it's worth it for you. Let's say you are paid $30 an hour and want a $400 set of headphones. That works out to be a little more than 13 hours' work. Do you still want those headphones?

- Find a buddy who's in a similar situation and make an agreement to keep each other accountable. If you're tempted to make a big purchase, talk to them first.

FAST FACT

YOU PROBABLY KNOW THAT MAKING ONLY THE MINIMUM REPAYMENTS ISN'T ENOUGH TO GET YOU OUT OF DEBT. BUT WHEN YOU LOOK AT THE INTEREST YOU'LL END UP PAYING, IT MIGHT BE ENOUGH TO SCARE YOU INTO ACTION. IF YOU HAD A $5,000 CREDIT CARD DEBT WITH AN INTEREST RATE OF 16.50% AND ONLY PAID THE MINIMUM REPAYMENTS, IT WOULD TAKE YOU MORE THAN 27 YEARS AND SEVEN MONTHS TO REPAY AND COST YOU $14,132 IN INTEREST!

ACTION PLAN

☐ *Stop using your credit card.*

☐ *Make a list of all your outstanding debts including interest rates and balance owing.*

☐ *Create a budget to work out how much you can put towards your debts each month.*

☐ *Talk to your lenders to see if you can negotiate a better rate.*

☐ *Consider your payment options – do you prefer the snowball or avalanche method?*

☐ *Think about whether you might find it easier to manage your repayments if you took up a balance transfer offer or consolidated the debt into a personal loan or your home loan.*

☐ *Talk to a financial counsellor if you think you could do with some extra help with your plan.*

☐ *After your debt is cleared, try to change your behaviour so that you don't end up in the same position.*

I CAN...

Deal
with curveballs

I always say that even though most of us have the best money intentions, life does throw us financial curveballs from time to time. It might be something 'small' such as car repairs or a dental emergency, or it might be something bigger like losing your job.

Ideally, you should be prepared for curveballs. As the saying goes: If you fail to plan, you plan to fail. That's why having an emergency fund is so important.

If you find yourself in a bit of a sticky situation without the safety net of an emergency fund, don't despair, as there are options.

Your 6-point plan to deal with curveballs

If you find yourself in crisis mode, here is my six-point plan to help you deal with any curveballs.

1. COUNT ALL YOUR BEANS

Figure out how much money you have to work with for budgeting purposes. Do you still have a regular income coming in or have you lost your job? Do you have enough savings to help you out of this bind?

If you're in need of a quick cash injection, take a look around the house to see if there is anything you may be able to sell that will put some money back in the coffers or maybe you can take on some odd jobs on Airtasker or become an Uber Eats driver to make some extra cash.

It's also worth exploring what financial support may be available to you (see Point 2).

One thing I don't recommend is selling your investments in a panic as a way to boost your income.

2. FIND OUT WHAT FINANCIAL SUPPORT MAY BE AVAILABLE

There are a number of government payments to help people in need. If you have lost your job you may be eligible for JobSeeker or Youth Allowance. Income and assets tests apply.

A word of warning, though. If you have received a lump sum payment, such as annual leave or redundancy, you may need to wait before you get a payment. You can still apply and you'll be told if you can get a payment, how much you'll get and what the waiting period will be.

If you are renting, check if you're eligible for Rent Assistance, which is an income top-up to make rent more affordable for low-income earners. You may be eligible if you receive certain payments already.

If you already receive some form of Centrelink income support, you may be eligible for an advance payment. This is essentially an interest-free loan available to people on a Centrelink income and is generally available twice every 12 months. You will repay the advance through fixed deductions from your fortnightly Centrelink payment.

There is a payments and services finder tool on the Services Australia website that can help you work out what payments you may be eligible for.

If you are after cash for emergency purchases such as a new fridge or car repairs, consider talking to not-for-profit organisation Good Shepherd Microfinance about the No Interest Loan Scheme (NILS). It provides loans up to $1,500, and repayments are arranged over 12 to 18 months. To be eligible you must have a healthcare or pension card, earn under $45,000, have lived in your current residence for three months, and have a willingness and capacity to repay the loan.

3. APPLY FOR ANY HARDSHIP RELIEF

It is worth talking to providers to find out if they can offer you a temporary reprieve to get you through a tough spot.

Your mortgage: Call your lender and talk to them about applying for a hardship variation. This usually comes in the form of 'pausing' your repayments. It is important to note, though, that interest will still be added to your mortgage so this option can end up costing you more in the long run. Other options may include increasing the loan term or temporarily switching to interest-only repayments.

Rent: If you are renting, talk to your landlord and/or real estate agent to explain your circumstances and ask if you can come to some sort of arrangement. Maybe they can reduce the rent temporarily and you can catch up later when you are in a better position.

Bills: If you can't pay your electricity, gas, phone or water bill, contact your service provider straightaway. They will explain your options, which may include a payment extension, paying in instalments, Centrelink deductions or applying for a utility rebate or voucher.

4. REVIEW YOUR SPENDING

Take a closer look at your expenses and group them into must-haves and nice-to-haves. Get rid of everything in the nice-to-have bucket. For example, if you pay someone for lawn care or dry cleaning, those are expenses you could temporarily put on pause.

Once you've cut the fluff from your budget, you can take a second look at your must-have spending and find ways to cut back. Even though some of our regular bills might seem small and insignificant on their own, collectively they can put an enormous amount of pressure on our budgets. Start by shopping around to find out if you can get a better deal or ask for discounts.

5. HIT PAUSE ON YOUR GOAL

Perhaps you're working to pay off your high-interest credit card debt this year or maybe your goal was to eliminate your student loan balances. Although setting financial goals is wise, there's nothing wrong with hitting the pause button in the middle of a crisis. Just remember to 'unpause' when the crisis passes.

6. VOW TO SET UP AN EMERGENCY FUND

When you get through this crisis, promise yourself that you'll set up an emergency fund. You'll definitely be glad you did if you find yourself in a similar predicament in the future.

THE COST OF BORROWING $1,000

Need $1,000? Here's a look at some of your options and how much it will cost if you repay it over three months.

NILS

$FREE

For essential goods and services only
Repayments can be made over 12-18 months.
Eligibility criteria applies

Source: nils.com.au

HOME LOAN REDRAW

$4.59

TOTAL COST

Redraw fee: Nil
Interest: $4.59
Fortnightly repayments: $167.43˙

*Source: canstar.com.au. Assumes interest rate of 3.41%pa. *Equivalent fortnightly repayment on borrowed amount.*

CREDIT CARD PURCHASE

$19.88

TOTAL COST

Interest: $19.88
Fortnightly repayments: $169.98

Source: canstar.com.au. Assumes purchase rate of 14.75%pa. Note annual fee may also apply.

CREDIT CARD CASH ADVANCE

$25.44

TOTAL COST

Interest: $25.44
Fortnightly repayments: $170.91

Source: canstar.com.au. Assumes cash advance rate of 18.86%pa. Note annual fee may also apply.

PAYDAY LOAN

$320

TOTAL COST

Establishment fee: $200
Monthly fees: $120
Fortnightly repayments: $188.57

Source: moneysmart.gov.au. Fees are set at the maximum a payday lender can charge. Establishment fee based on 20% of amount borrowed and monthly fees at 4% each month.

Building an emergency fund

Having money stashed away can make life less stressful when expensive surprises crop up. That way you won't have to rely on credit cards or other loans to get you out of trouble.

It can be hard to put money away regularly if you're just trying to get by but, ideally, you should make it a priority.

Look for areas where you can cut back and redirect that money towards your emergency fund. You might also consider selling unwanted items and using the money you make to top up your emergency fund, and if you get a windfall such as a tax refund, pop that into your rainy day fund as well.

How much should you have in your fund?

At the very least you should aim to have a few thousand dollars in there, but most experts recommend having between three and six months' worth of expenses stashed away. You can include only the expenses that form your bare-bones budget such as rent/mortgage, food, utilities and so on, but that can still add up and it will probably take some time to accumulate.

Let's say you estimate your monthly expenses come to about $5,000, then you would be aiming to have between $15,000 and $30,000 in your emergency fund.

If you can save $200 a month it would take a little more than six years to save $15,000; if you can save $500 a month, you'd hit that $15,000 goal in two and a half years.

Where to keep your emergency fund

The money needs to be easily accessible so that you can get your hands on it fairly quickly when you need it.

Ideally, you should have it in a separate savings account – and one that is paying a decent rate. When you have worked out how much you can save each pay, make sure you pay yourself first.

Set up regular automatic direct debits from your everyday account into your savings. Time the transfers to coincide with paydays to avoid overdrawing your transaction account.

If you have a home loan, you may consider putting the money into an offset account if you have one linked to your home loan. This will help reduce the interest you pay on your mortgage because the money in this account 'offsets' the amount you owe on your mortgage, and you'll only be charged interest on the difference.

If you don't have an offset account but have redraw, you may still opt to add it to your mortgage. Be sure to read the fine print about your redraw facility.

When should you use it?

Remember the money is for emergencies: your car breaks down, you need a new fridge, or you lose your job. Don't be tempted to dip into it for things that don't fall into that category, such as a weekend away or a new laptop. Also, if you do take money out of your emergency fund, make sure you top it up again as soon as you can.

ACTION PLAN

☐ *Work out how much money you have coming in and look for ways you may be able to boost it.*

☐ *Find out what additional support you may be eligible for from the government or not-for-profit groups such as Good Shepherd.*

☐ *Talk to your lenders, landlord and utility companies about any hardship relief they may be able to offer.*

☐ *Preserve your cash flow by sticking to minimum repayments and cashing in reward points to pay for non-essentials.*

☐ *Hit pause on any financial goals you have set yourself for now.*

☐ *Focus on building an emergency fund to help you deal with any future curveballs.*

Life moves fast and you want a lot out of it. You want to be able to afford a car, you want amazing holidays, and you want to be able to buy a home. And, after you have bought a home, you might start thinking about how you'd like to renovate it. You can have it all … it's just a matter of putting a plan in place. In this section, you'll be given the facts, figures and strategies to help you tick off life's key financial milestones – and get to enjoy your purchases without being a slave to your lifestyle.

PART III

TICK OFF THOSE LIFE MILESTONES

—

I CAN...

Buy a car

There is a lot to love about owning a car. It means no more crowded public transport, no more waiting for an Uber, just the freedom to get up and go – where you want, when you want.

A car could also be one of the most expensive purchases you'll ever make, second only to a home. So, along with the fun parts like choosing the make and model, going for a few test drives, and picking your favourite colour, it's also important to work out how you're going to pay for it. And the initial price tag is just the beginning.

Budget for your car

Budgeting for a car doesn't simply mean deciding how much you can afford to pay upfront. Cars come with running costs, and it's worth having an idea of what you could be up for on a regular basis. Along with fuel, you need to allow for rego, servicing, a new set of tyres every few years, and insurance. I'll take a closer look at car cover later on but, at a minimum, budget for compulsory third party (CTP) cover.

An easy way to compare the ongoing costs of different cars is by heading to the websites of motoring associations like NRMA and RACV, which crunch the numbers to work out the running costs of different makes and models. As a guide, a new Volkswagen Polo, with a price tag of around $25,000, can set you back $149 in weekly running costs. A bigger car, like a new Subaru Liberty, with a price tag of $35,000, can come with weekly running costs of around $200. The $51 weekly difference between the two may not sound like much but it adds up to $2,652 over the course of year or an extra $13,260 over five years. To be fair, these costs assume a car loan charging 6.17% interest – you may pay less. They also include depreciation, which doesn't come out of your hip pocket. But the bottom line is that your budget needs to be able to manage all the costs associated with the car of your choice.

Paying for it all – save the cash or borrow?

Taking the time to save for a car means you won't have to worry about loan repayments or interest costs. But unless you opt for a cheapie used car, it's going to take time to accumulate the funds needed.

The crazy thing is that offering to pay in cash is unlikely to see you score a discount at the car yard. The big dealerships all offer in-house finance and they can make more money if you take out finance with them. This being the case – and with interest rates being so low these days – financing your car will let you own a set of wheels sooner. And, if you plan to use the car for work-related activities, you may be able to claim all or part of the loan interest on tax, which pushes the cost down.

Car finance options

There are three main options to finance your car – a loan, dealer finance, and a novated lease. The key with each is to weigh up the pros and cons.

CAR LOANS Car loans are a super-simple product. You borrow a set amount, make repayments for a set term, usually one to seven years, often at a fixed interest rate, which makes the loan easy to budget for. Then, at the end of the loan, you own the car outright with no more to pay. Simple.

Even better, plenty of lenders offer car loans, so be prepared to look beyond your regular bank. This is one area where credit unions and smaller, member-owned banks offer very competitive deals. Some even offer flexible loan features like extra repayments at no charge to help clear the debt sooner, and free redraw if you need to withdraw some of those additional payments in an emergency.

As a guide, in August 2020, the cheapest secured car loan on comparison site Canstar's database was with Queensland Country Credit Union at 2.99%. By contrast, with some of the big banks, you could pay anywhere from 6.99% to upwards of 9.99%.

The lowest rates apply to secured loans, which means stumping up your car as security. That may seem like a formality but if you can't keep up the repayments, the lender has the right to repossess the car. Most lenders won't accept cars aged more than five years as security. If you're buying an older car, this can narrow the choice to an unsecured personal loan and will likely mean paying a higher rate, in some cases around 12%.

Use the comparison rate

The interest rate isn't the only cost of a car loan. Most lenders charge an upfront loan establishment fee, often around $200-$250. The thing to watch for is monthly loan fees. Not all lenders charge these, but paying just $12 a month can add an extra $720 to the cost of a five-year loan. Take the example of that 2.99% secured car loan. It charges both an application fee of $120 and ongoing fee of $60, which means its comparison rate jumps up to 3.60% on a $30,000 car loan over five years.

This is why it's important to look at the comparison rate, not just the headline rate, when weighing up different loans. The comparison rate includes most upfront and ongoing fees, giving you a clearer picture of the true cost of a loan.

Ask about car loan pre-approval

The last thing you need is to commit to buying a car only to find you can't get a loan for the price you've agreed to pay. The best way around this is to have your loan pre-approved. This means a lender has given your loan a thumbs-up, though final approval will depend on the car you buy and whether your income has changed since pre-approval was granted.

The beauty of pre-approval is that it lets you know how much you can afford to spend on a car, and that's a big plus for setting a buying limit at the car yard.

DEALER FINANCE The minute you set foot in a car yard the dealer is going to invest time convincing you to buy a vehicle. And they want to seal the deal by making finance as effortless as possible. That's where the appeal of car yard finance lies – it can be easy to arrange.

Dealer finance often gets a bad rap, but to be fair the big dealerships can offer competitive interest rates. The problem lies in lack of transparency. Car makers' websites are packed with glossy images but they're light on the nitty gritty of financing costs.

It's often only when you're sitting across the table from the dealership's finance manager that the details are discussed. Even then, the focus can be on how much you'll pay each month rather than the interest rate involved. So be prepared to ask what the rate is inclusive of upfront and ongoing fees – in other words, the comparison rate.

Watch for 'balloon' payments

Perhaps the biggest trap of dealer finance is 'balloon' payments. These are not the sort of balloons you find at parties. A balloon payment is a lump sum payment made at the end of the loan term. It can come as a real shock to find that after years of diligently paying off your car, you still need to pay several thousand dollars just to own the vehicle outright.

10.4

THE AVERAGE AGE, IN YEARS, OF VEHICLES ACROSS AUSTRALIA, ACCORDING TO THE AUSTRALIAN BUREAU OF STATISTICS.

Car dealers will argue that balloon payments make it possible to offer a low interest rate. But it can also be a way to keep business ticking over. Unless you've saved a lump sum of cash, it can seem like a good idea to trade in the car for a newer model and roll the balloon payment over to a new loan. However, this just sets you on the treadmill for several more years of repayments with yet another balloon owing at some point in the future.

The main point is to check if there is a balloon payment. If the answer is "yes", ask yourself if you really want to go down that road.

NOVATED LEASING There is a third way to pay for a car and that's through leasing. I don't mean renting your car. I'm talking about a 'novated' lease, which involves using salary sacrifice to pay for your car with before-tax income.

A novated lease is a three-way arrangement between a finance company, your employer and you, as an employee. Your boss agrees to pay the car lease payments – and in most cases the vehicle's running costs – out of your pre-tax salary. It can be a very tax-friendly way to pay for a car. The catch is that when your employer pays for your car, the Australian Tax Office (ATO) regards it as a fringe benefit, and this can see fringe benefits tax (FBT) levied against your employer.

Even the most supportive boss is unlikely to pay an extra 47% tax (the rate of FBT) for you to enjoy tax-friendly car finance. The way around this is for you to contribute to the cost of FBT, and this is usually done through a mix of before- and after-tax 'employee contributions'. This may seem counter-productive but as Table 1 on page 74 shows, it can reduce or eliminate the impact of FBT, and still let you come out in front financially.

To see how a novated lease can work, let's say Suzi is an employee earning $86,000 annually – approximately the average adult full-time wage. She wants to buy a car costing $45,000, and she can either take out a car loan at 6% or finance the vehicle through a novated lease. The car's running costs, including comprehensive insurance and finance, come to $13,995 annually.

Looking at Table 1, it's easy to see how paying for the car's costs before tax through a novated lease will leave Suzi $1,131 better off each year compared to paying for the car – including loan finance – using after-tax money. I realise the numbers are complicated, but your payroll officer or the finance company will do the sums for you – you don't have to do the calculations yourself. It's also a good idea to run it past your accountant.

The downsides of novated leases

The key catch of a novated lease is that when your lease term ends, you won't own the car unless you make a lump sum 'residual' payment. The ATO sets the value of the residual – and the longer your lease, the lower the residual will be.

TABLE 1 **NOVATED LEASE VS CAR LOAN**

	NOVATED LEASE	CAR LOAN
Gross annual salary	$86,000	$86,000
Annual finance costs before tax	$4,855	-
Employee contribution before tax	$831	-
Taxable salary	$80,314	$86,000
Income tax (plus Medicare)	$19,255	$21,217
After-tax salary	$61,059	$64,783
After-tax employee contribution	$9,140	-
Annual car running costs	-	$13,995
Take home pay after tax & car costs	$51,919	$50,788
Annual saving of novated lease	$1,131	

Source: Toyota Fleet Management. Assumes lease term of five years, interest rate of 6.0%, 20,000km annually, and 0% business use.

But even at the end of a five-year novated lease, the minimum residual value will be equal to 28.13% of the vehicle's original purchase price. So, after five years of making lease payments you still owe more than one-quarter of the car's original value, which could be more than the car's market value.

If you have the cash, you could choose to pay the residual. In reality, many employees roll their lease over to a new car and continue with the novated arrangement. At some stage, though, you need to address how you will pay the residual if you want to own a car outright.

The other drawback is that if you lose your job, the 'novated' aspect of your lease ends, meaning the employer doesn't make the car payments – you do. It's possible to protect against this risk by taking out redundancy insurance or car lease cover but it is another cost to wear. Bear in mind, employers don't have to agree to a novated lease, so there are no guarantees your next boss will go along with the arrangement.

Which is better – new or used?

Few things beat the feeling of buckling yourself into a brand-new car while you gaze lovingly at an odometer with next to no kilometres. But it's a buzz that comes with a price. New cars will cost more than a similar used vehicle. And make no mistake, cars are a terrible investment. The minute you drive a new car out of the showroom, it plunges in value.

In fact, according to the NRMA, cars can lose one-third of their value in the first three years alone. That's a serious premium to pay for the pleasure of owning a new vehicle, although there are ways to slow the rate of depreciation. Popular makes and models tend to be better at holding their value. Fuel-efficient cars generally depreciate at a slower rate than gas guzzlers, and taking good care of your car through garaging and regular servicing will help it hold its value for longer.

If you're happy to wear the cost of depreciation, new cars have plenty of upsides. You can expect years of hassle-free driving backed by a warranty extending generally from three to five years. Insurance premiums tend to be cheaper; loan finance for new cars usually comes with lower interest rates and you won't need to organise a rego check for the first five years.

If you're after a more budget-friendly option, a decent second-hand car can fit the bill. The upfront price will be lower, but there are plenty of sharks out there and you need to be wary of buying someone else's

10 FEATURES TO CONSIDER
WHEN BUYING A CAR

These days cars have so many features. Some help keep you safe
while others make driving more enjoyable. Take a look at some
of the features you may want to check out when shopping
for your new car.

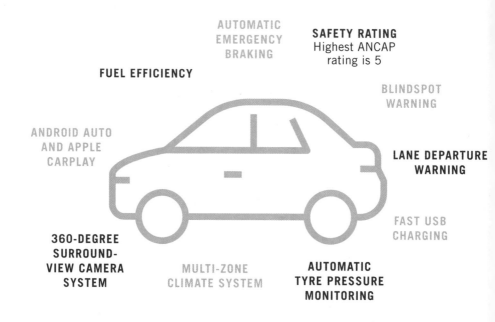

AUTOMATIC
EMERGENCY
BRAKING

SAFETY RATING
Highest ANCAP
rating is 5

FUEL EFFICIENCY

BLINDSPOT
WARNING

ANDROID AUTO
AND APPLE
CARPLAY

**LANE DEPARTURE
WARNING**

FAST USB
CHARGING

**360-DEGREE
SURROUND-
VIEW CAMERA
SYSTEM**

MULTI-ZONE
CLIMATE SYSTEM

**AUTOMATIC
TYRE PRESSURE
MONITORING**

problem. Unless you're thoroughly up to speed on mechanics – and can pick a crankshaft from a carburetor – it's a good idea to organise a pre-purchase car check through your state motoring association. It's a service that can cost $300 with the likes of NRMA (less if you become a member), but it can be money well spent.

If you find a car you like that's being sold privately, it is critical to do a PPSR check. Just jump onto ppsr.gov.au, which will take you to the Personal Property Securities Register. This is a national database that shows if a car has been written off, stolen or still has money owing on it. It only costs $2 to do a PPSR check and it really is a must-do.

If a debt is registered against a vehicle, the finance company has a right to turn up at any time and repossess it, even after you've paid for the car. Do not take the seller's word that any outstanding finance has been paid off. It is up to you, the buyer, to confirm with the finance company that the debt has been cleared. With plenty of other used cars up for grabs, it could be a lot easier to walk away from the deal.

If you're buying a pre-loved car, ideally aim for a vehicle that's between three to five years' old. The worst of the car's depreciation will be behind it, you should still be able to land a competitive rate on finance, and if the car has been well-maintained, it will hopefully give you many years of enjoyment on the open road.

Insuring your new set of wheels

Now that you have your car, you need to protect it. Plenty can go wrong on and off the road, which is why Compulsory Third Party (CTP or Green Slip) insurance is a must-have before you can even register a car.

CTP covers you against personal injury you cause to someone else in an accident. In NSW, Qld, SA and the ACT, drivers can choose their CTP insurer. This provides an opportunity to shop around and save on premiums, although there's usually not much in it between different insurers. In other states, CTP is organised through a single state-owned or government-licensed insurer.

While CTP is a must-have, it doesn't protect your car or someone else's car/property in a bingle. If you have a fender bender and you're at fault, CTP won't cover the bill. One option is to take out third party property insurance. This provides a payout if you damage someone else's property – be it their car, mailbox or fence. But the payout won't cover damage to your own car.

Having gone to all the trouble of buying and paying for a car of your own, you'd be crazy not to take out comprehensive car insurance especially if the car is under finance. Comprehensive really is the gold standard in car insurance. You'll be covered if your car is stolen or damaged by wild weather like hail or rain, and you're covered for damage in an accident no matter who is at fault.

The premiums for comprehensive insurance are based on where you live, your age, and the make, model and age of your car. Another factor that determines the cost is whether you insure the car for its market value or opt for an agreed value. The premiums are likely to be lower if you select market value because your car will depreciate over time. On the flipside, the certainty of an agreed value policy can be very reassuring especially if your car is still under finance.

ACTION PLAN

☐ *Work out your budget and how much you can afford to pay for a car. As well as the upfront costs, consider the ongoing running costs.*

☐ *Start saving money towards your purchase as ideally it is better to pay for at least some of it yourself.*

☐ *If you will need to borrow money to buy a car, start exploring your finance options.*

☐ *Think about whether you want a brand-new car or a second-hand vehicle.*

☐ *Research cars that may be suitable.*

☐ *Start shopping around. Classified sites such as carsales.com.au and carsguide.com.au can be a good place to begin your search.*

☐ *If you're buying a used car, it's a good idea to get a pre-purchase mechanical inspection and also search the Personal Property Securities Register (PPSR).*

☐ *If you're buying a new or demo vehicle, check out the details of the warranty.*

☐ *Negotiate the price – make sure you have done your research to determine a fair price.*

☐ *Before you drive away take out insurance.*

I CAN...

Go on holidays

It's always nice to have something to look forward to and a holiday certainly fits that description. Organising a trip and thinking about all the fun and exciting things you'll see and do can be almost (emphasis on the almost) as fun as the holiday itself.

Overseas travel might look a little different for a while as a result of the pandemic but there's still plenty to explore in our own backyard in the meantime. This is an ideal time to start planning and saving for your next adventure.

Set your budget

The best way to pay for a holiday is to save money first, but not everyone does. Research by credit bureau Experian found that more than half of Aussies put up to $4,000 on their credit card to pay for a holiday but only 37% paid it off immediately.

If you put a $4,000 holiday on a credit card charging 16.5%pa interest and you repaid $150 a month, you'd end up paying $931 in interest and it would take you two years and nine months to repay the holiday debt. Even if you upped your repayments to $300 a month, it would cost you $382 in interest.

To start saving, it's a good idea to set your holiday budget. To give you an idea, a one-week trip to New York costs approximately $2,275 per person, according to website budgetyourtrip.com, which collects data from travellers to come up with averages. This doesn't include airfares but does include accommodation, local transport, food, entertainment, tips and tours.

It's important to do your own research to get an idea of what your holiday will cost. The internet makes the entire process pretty simple, with information right at your fingertips.

Your biggest expenses will probably be your airfare (assuming you're flying) and accommodation. Then you need to factor in money for food, public transport, tours, shopping and other activities. This will vary depending on your destination as well as whether you want a budget holiday, something more comfortable, or you want to go all out. It could cost you anywhere between $100-$300 a day per person.

After you have set a budget, think about when you want to go, and work backwards to figure out how much you need to save from each pay to reach your goal. So, let's say you estimate your dream holiday will set you back $10,000 and you want to go in 12 months – that means you'd need to put away $384.62 a fortnight. It's important to arrange for that amount to be automatically transferred to a separate holiday account before you get your hands on it.

WHERE TO PUT YOUR SAVINGS

Given that you'll probably want to access the money in a relatively short time, it's probably best to leave the money in cash.

Your main options are an online saver or a notice saver. An online saver generally charges no fees and to deposit or withdraw money you need to transact online by transferring money to and from a specified traditional account. Often they have introductory promotional rates available to new customers for a limited period.

A notice saver generally doesn't charge fees, but your money is locked away so you can't access it on a whim, which is ideal if you find it hard to avoid temptation. To take out money, you need to give the institution notice. You can choose the period you like – 31-day, 60-day and 90-day options are generally available. You can add to your savings whenever you want.

When weighing up your options, consider the interest rate (including any promo rate), whether there are any fees, and how you will be accessing your money.

12-MONTH HOLIDAY SAVING PLAN

Breaking your savings goal into smaller chunks can make it feel more achievable. Take a look at how much you need to put away each fortnight or month to reach your goal.

IF YOU WANT THIS MUCH	SAVE THIS MUCH EACH FORTNIGHT	SAVE THIS MUCH EACH MONTH
$1,000	$38.46	$83.33
$2,000	$76.92	$166.67
$3,000	$115.38	$250.00
$4,000	$153.85	$333.33
$5,000	$192.31	$416.67
$6,000	$230.77	$500.00
$7,000	$269.23	$583.33
$8,000	$307.69	$666.67
$9,000	$346.15	$750.00
$10,000	$384.62	$833.33

LAY-BY HOLIDAYS

Another option you might want to consider using to pay for your trip is lay-by. This involves making a deposit and then paying off the trip in instalments. The trip will be paid for before you leave and you won't have to pay any interest. Some of the companies offering this type of option include Pay Later Travel and Play Travel, which is an Afterpay service. Some travel agents offer similar arrangements.

One advantage of lay-by holidays is that you lock in the cost now, which may help protect you from future price hikes. On the flipside, though, prices may be higher when you use these services than if you were to book directly with an airline, but that would mean having available funds. It is a bit of a catch-22. It's important to do your research and crunch the numbers.

If you're thinking about using this approach, some of the questions to ask include:

- How much deposit do I need to pay?
- How long do I have to pay it all off and what happens if I am not able to pay it off in that time frame?
- Are there any fees?
- What happens if I miss an instalment or pay late?
- What happens if I want to cancel?
- Can I make changes to my booking?

TIPS TO HELP YOU SAVE MONEY

A great trip doesn't have to cost you a fortune. Here are some ideas that may help you save money.

- Book in advance. You may be able to score a great deal. Data from Skyscanner shows that booking flights 22 weeks in advance to international destinations is the optimum time to get the greatest savings. For domestic flights it's 21 weeks.

- Travel during off-peak periods. Flights and accommodation tend to be cheaper and you won't have to deal with big crowds.

- Book directly with the airline or hotel and chances are you'll get a better deal. Just make sure to shop around and compare prices first.

- Be flexible with your travel dates. Even opting to travel a few days sooner or later could net you savings. Many airlines' websites give you the option to search this way.

- Consider house swapping, where you temporarily exchange homes with another traveller.

TRAVEL INSURANCE

Travel insurance is a must – especially if you're heading overseas. Sometimes plans go awry, and travel insurance can help compensate you if, for example, you have to cancel your trip because of illness, your luggage goes missing or you need medical treatment overseas.

First check if you have complimentary travel insurance on your credit card. Ask your credit card provider if you're unsure. Generally, you need to pay for part or all of your trip on your credit card for insurance to apply.

There are quite a few providers offering travel insurance so it's important to shop around. It's advisable to take out cover when you buy your ticket. If not, you probably won't be covered if you need to cancel your trip. Don't base your decision solely on price.

Whether you are considering using the insurance on your credit card or taking out a separate policy, it's vital to find out what is and isn't covered. This is a lesson many people learnt as a result of the coronavirus pandemic. Keep in mind that there are some standard general exclusions in most policies, such as war and acts of terrorism, self-inflicted injury, unattended luggage and loss of cash.

It's worth noting also that generally you'll only be covered for cancellation costs in certain situations, such as illness or the death of a close relative, but not if you change your mind. You may be able to pay extra for a policy that covers you for change of mind.

'Dangerous activities' such as rock climbing may also be excluded or you may be able to buy separate cover.

Check any limits on how much you'll be paid. For example, you'll generally be covered for loss of personal luggage and belongings, but find out what the maximum payout would be. The same goes for medical expenses, which can be very high.

TRAVEL MONEY

Another decision you need to make before travelling overseas is how you plan to pay for things when you're there. The main options are cash, a debit card linked to your transaction account, your credit card or a travel money card. You might choose to use a combination of all four.

It's very important to pay close attention to any fees because they can quickly add up. These may include currency conversion fees and ATM withdrawal fees. And prepaid travel money cards may charge you a fee for loading or reloading the card.

One of the advantages of travel money cards is that you lock in the exchange rate when you load the money so you don't have to worry about currency fluctuations.

On the flipside Canstar's analysis has found that the exchange rates available on credit and debit cards tend to be more favourable than those on travel money cards.

FAST FACT

MAY IS THE CHEAPEST MONTH TO TRAVEL, WITH AVERAGE SAVINGS OF 13% TO ALL MAJOR INTERNATIONAL AND DOMESTIC DESTINATIONS, ACCORDING TO SKYSCANNER.

ACTION PLAN

- [ ] *Start thinking about where you would like to go.*
- [ ] *Work out how much your trip will cost.*
- [ ] *Make a plan to start saving money regularly to reach your savings goal.*
- [ ] *Open a separate account for your holiday savings.*
- [ ] *Book your flights and accommodation.*
- [ ] *Take out travel insurance.*
- [ ] *Make sure your passport and any necessary visas are in order if you're heading overseas.*
- [ ] *If you're travelling internationally, organise your travel money.*

I CAN...

Buy a house

The great Aussie dream of owning your own home still exists, but it may feel unattainable for many people. I have to admit I was pretty fortunate – I bought my first property with the help of Mum and Dad. And given that it was almost 30 years ago, prices were affordable compared to what they are today. I know that my kids will not have it as easy. That said, buying a house is not an impossible task – it just may require some sacrifices.

1. Start saving your deposit

One of the biggest challenges for aspiring homeowners is saving for a deposit. To buy a $500,000 home, you'd need to save between $25,000 and $100,000, depending on whether you're aiming for a 5% or 20% deposit. That's before you factor in all the extra costs associated with buying a home such as stamp duty, legal fees, inspections and possibly lenders mortgage insurance (LMI).

To help you work out how much of a deposit to aim for you need to at least have an idea of how much you want to spend on a house, and whether you are happy to pay LMI, and budget for the extra expenses (more on this later).

You'll generally need at least 5% of the purchase price to be able to get a loan. If you do borrow more than 80% of the property's value, it will mean that you have to pay LMI. This doesn't protect you – it protects the lender if you default on your loan. And it isn't cheap.

To give you an idea: If you had saved $40,000 for a $500,000 property, LMI would set you back $11,530, according to the premium estimator on the Genworth website. Save $30,000 more and the LMI premium would come down to $4,768. You can pay it upfront or you can add it to your home loan, but you'll have to pay interest.

Now you may think it's better to save a bigger deposit rather than forking out extra money for LMI, but it can sometimes pay to jump into the market sooner. I discuss this scenario in detail in Chapter 19: Should I buy now and pay LMI or wait until I have a 20% deposit?

AVOIDING LMI There are ways you may be able to avoid LMI. One example is the government's First Home Loan Deposit Scheme (FHLDS), which provides a guarantee to participating lenders that will allow eligible first home buyers to purchase a home with a deposit of as little as 5% and without needing to pay for LMI. You'll have to meet eligibility requirements such as an income test and there are caps on the price of the property. There are also limited spots available.

Another way you may be able to boost your deposit – and potentially avoid LMI – is with the help of family. Could your parents or other relatives give you enough money to get your deposit to 20%? Of course, handing out cash might not be an option for all families, but maybe they can act as guarantor if they own their own home. Essentially, as a guarantor they will put up the equity in their own home as additional security for your loan.

It's important that your family understands the implications, though: The lender can turn to them to pay up if you fall behind on repayments.

THE HIDDEN COSTS OF BUYING A HOME Saving enough money for a deposit is just one part of the equation. You'll also need money to cover the upfront expenses, which can easily add an extra 5%-7% to the cost.

Stamp duty is likely to be the biggest expense. It will vary depending on where the property is located, as it's a state government tax. You may be able to get a stamp duty concession if you're a first-home buyer, though – again the rules vary between states and territories.

The graphic on page 91 looks at some of the other expenses to consider.

HIDDEN COSTS OF BUYING A PROPERTY

Here is an example of the upfront costs of buying a $700,000 property in Victoria with a 10% deposit.

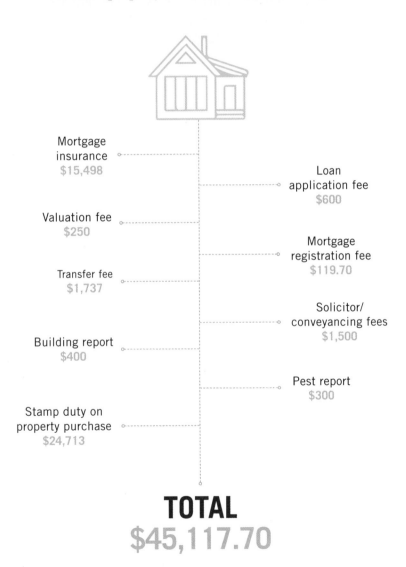

Mortgage insurance
$15,498

Loan application fee
$600

Valuation fee
$250

Mortgage registration fee
$119.70

Transfer fee
$1,737

Solicitor/ conveyancing fees
$1,500

Building report
$400

Pest report
$300

Stamp duty on property purchase
$24,713

TOTAL
$45,117.70

MAKE A PLAN TO SAVE When you have worked out your goal amount it can be a good idea to work backwards; that way you'll know how much you should be putting away each month to reach your goal. For example, if you are aiming to save a $50,000 deposit in five years, you'd have to save about $833 a month. But if you were hoping to reach your goal in three years, you'd need to put away $1,389 a month!

Getting your foot on the property ladder may require some sacrifices and they may have to start now. To maximise the amount you can stash away each month, look for ways that you can cut costs or bring in extra cash.

WHERE TO STASH YOUR SAVINGS There are a few different places to put your savings including savings accounts, ETFs, managed funds, using the First Home Super Saver Scheme (FHSSS) or a combination of all of the above.

Some of the factors to consider when deciding on the best option for you include the amount you have saved already, how much you can save on a regular basis, the time frame you are looking at and the level of risk you are willing to take.

Online savings accounts are probably the lowest-risk option because the government guarantees deposits of up to $250,000 in authorised deposit-taking institutions. Unfortunately, right now many are paying only slightly more than what you'd be getting by storing money under the mattress!

I personally am a fan of mix-and-match strategies when it comes to saving for a home deposit. A little in cash to keep things safe and a little in high-growth investments like shares if you've got the time and risk appetite for a potential bigger return.

I also like having cash in the asset class I want to buy – in this case property. This way, if property goes up so does your balance (and conversely if property goes down so does your balance).

Options include fractional property investing platform BrickX or exchange traded funds (ETFs) that give you exposure to property.

You can read more about BrickX in Chapter 11: I can invest with just $100 a week. For more on ETFs, head to Chapter 13: I can choose my own ETFs.

If you opt for investments with exposure to the sharemarket, it's important to be aware that they are higher risk than cash in the bank, so if the market falls your deposit will go backwards. You will need to take a long-term view of at least five years to ride out any volatility.

It's also important to factor in brokerage fees if you are using ETFs. It's a good idea to place savings in an online account first, then to transfer the funds to buy into the ETF when you've got a larger amount. Doing it this way will reduce the impact of fees on your savings.

Then there's the FHSSS. It allows you to make voluntary contributions into your super fund to save for your first home. You can then apply to release your voluntary contributions, along with associated earnings, to help you purchase your first home. You can add up to $15,000 in one financial year, or $30,000 in total.

The benefit of saving through your super is that your before-tax contributions as well as the investment returns are taxed at only 15%, which is probably less than your marginal tax rate.

FIRST HOME OWNER GRANT If you are buying your first home, you may be able to get some free cash from the government as a helping hand. The size of the grant and the eligibility criteria vary from state to state and, in many cases, it may only be available if you are buying a brand-new home that has never been lived in, or building an entirely new one.

In NSW, for example, you may be able to get $10,000 if you are buying or building your first home, it's a new home that no-one has lived in before and it's worth no more than $750,000.

You may also be eligible for a discount on stamp duty as a first-time buyer. The grants and discounts are managed by state and territory governments so it's best to check with your state revenue office for details.

2. Set your budget

The next step is to set your budget. You need to factor in the following three things:

HOW MUCH HAVE YOU SAVED? This is what we have talked about – the amount you have saved for your deposit as well as the extra costs that come with buying a house. You can also include the First Home Owner Grant amount if you are eligible, as well as any financial support you may have received from your family.

HOW MUCH CAN YOU BORROW? You may think you can get a loan for $600,000 but would a lender agree? There are online calculators that can give you an estimate but it's best to talk to a lender or mortgage broker to get a more realistic idea.

HOW MUCH CAN YOU AFFORD? It's important to do your own calculations to work out how much you can afford to borrow. Estimate your repayments based on different loan amounts and also factor in a buffer. Rates will not be this low forever so it's important to be confident that you'll still be able to afford the repayments if rates were to go up by 2%-3%.

To give you an idea if you were to borrow $600,000 over 25 years at a rate of 3%, your repayments would be $2,845 a month. That might sound manageable. But if rates went up to 5.5% then you'd have to pay an extra $840 a month! Is that still an amount you can afford?

Also keep in mind that owning a home comes with expenses that you don't have to worry about as a tenant, such as council and water rates, repairs and maintenance. So, you'll need to budget for those as well.

3. Get your finances sorted

So, you've saved the deposit, have an idea of how much you can afford and want to buy – the next step is getting a loan. There are a number of different types of loans but the four main options are:

BASIC/NO-FRILLS VARIABLE RATE A variable rate loan with a relatively low interest rate and minimal features. Check whether you can make additional repayments and repay the loan early without being penalised, and find out what features are excluded. These days there's not that much difference between a basic loan and a standard variable rate.

STANDARD VARIABLE RATE This is probably the most popular type of loan. It offers a few more features and flexibility but at a slightly higher rate than a basic loan. The main difference between the two is that generally you'll have both offset and redraw facilities on a standard loan.

FIXED RATE The interest rate is set for a particular term – usually one to five years. That means your repayments are set for that period. Ask if you can make extra repayments and if so whether a limit applies.

PACKAGE LOAN This involves combining your home loan and other financial products into one bundle. You will have to pay an annual fee of about $300-$400, but you'll get rate discounts (usually around 0.7%), reduced ongoing fees, fee-free credit cards and transaction accounts.

Comparing loans

Here are some of the factors to consider when comparing loans.

INTEREST RATE The interest rate is no doubt one of the most important considerations. There can be a huge variation between the cheapest and most expensive loans. Comparison sites such as Canstar, of which I am Editor-of-Large, can be a good place to start as you can get a better idea of what a good rate is.

FEES You should also take a look at the fees, which can include application and establishment fees and annual or monthly fees, as well as valuation and settlement fees. You may be surprised at what an impact fees can have on the cost of the loan. High fees can make a low-rate loan more expensive than a higher-rate loan with no or few fees.

To get a true picture of the cost of the loan, you should consider the 'comparison rate' or AAPR. You'll generally find this on a lender's website and it takes the fees into account as well as the rate.

LOAN FEATURES I always say that the cheapest loan won't necessarily be the best one for you. You need to think about the features you want in your mortgage. Here are a few popular ones to consider.

Redraw or offset: Redraw and offset are probably among the more in-demand features, partly because they can both help you reduce the interest you pay on your loan. You don't need a loan with both – just one or the other.

With redraw, you can make additional repayments on your loan but access the money if you need it. If you are considering redraw, make sure you ask if there is a minimum redraw amount and if there are any fees to use the service.

It's also worth noting that most mortgage contracts give lenders the right to cancel features such as redraw. This would normally only happen if you were in arrears or your circumstances drastically changed.

Offset works in a similar way, but any extra money sits in a separate account linked to your mortgage rather than going straight onto the loan. Any money sitting in that account is offset against your loan balance, reducing the interest payable. Traditionally, loans with an offset facility have been a little more expensive but that gap has started closing.

50%

OF AUSSIES AGED 30-34 OWNED A HOME, ACCORDING TO 2016 CENSUS DATA – DOWN FROM 64% IN 1971.

Split: This means you can have part of your loan as fixed and the rest as variable, letting you hedge your bets on how you think rates will go.

Top-up: This lets you add to your existing loan if there is adequate equity – a good option for funding renovations. See Chapter 10: I can pay for renos.

Portability: This feature means you can take the loan with you when you sell your house and buy another one. It can save you time and the costs of refinancing, but fees may still apply to use the feature so be sure to find out what they would be.

Repayment holiday: This means you may be able to 'pause' your home loan under certain circumstances – the most common is if you've had a baby and you're on parental leave, but it may also be available if you can't work for a while or experience hardship. Some lenders may only let you take a repayment holiday if you're ahead in your repayments.

It's important to note that interest will still be charged during the repayment-free period, and as a result interest is capitalised and you'll end up paying more over the life of the loan.

This might seem very overwhelming, in which case you may want to chat to a mortgage broker. They can help you identify how much you can borrow, the types of features you might find useful and loans that would suit your needs – and they'll take care of all the paperwork. There is more information on mortgage brokers in Chapter 17: I can find good advice.

APPLYING FOR A LOAN Before you go house-hunting, it's important to get pre-approval from a lender so you know exactly how much money you have to play with.

It's worth noting that pre-approval generally lasts for three to six months. Find out what will happen if you don't find a home you want in that time frame. The pre-approval may be extended for a fee but there's also a chance you will need to go through the application process again.

When you're ready to apply for a home loan, expect to be asked a lot of questions and to provide a lot of paperwork to support your request. Your income will be one thing lenders will look at but there will be a host of other considerations such as your expenses and employment history.

Here are a few tips to help you boost your chances of getting your loan approved:

• The bigger the deposit the better.

• Clean up your spending in the lead-up to applying for a loan. Stick to a budget and limit any non-essential spending.

- Reduce your outstanding debts as much as possible or consider consolidating them into the home loan that you're applying for.

- Cancel any credit cards you don't use, or at the very least reduce the credit limits, as that can boost your borrowing power.

- Get a copy of your credit file to make sure there are no black marks you're not aware of that could hurt your chances of securing a loan.

4. Find your first home

Now comes the fun part – house hunting. Well, it might be fun in the beginning but it can get tedious once you've been visiting open houses for months and keep missing out on properties.

So where do you start? Location, location, location! I know it's a cliché but there's a reason for that. When deciding on a location think about, among other things, whether it has the facilities and amenities you need, for example, schools, parks and restaurants. What are the public transport options like? Is it close to family and friends?

Don't get your heart set on one particular suburb. It's best to look at a broader area and research the various suburbs in that region. You might find more affordable options that way. If you're not already living in the area, spend a few weekends there – check out the shops, eat at the restaurants, visit the pubs to get a better idea of whether it's a good fit.

It also pays to think about whether it's an area people will want to live in, in the future. Realistically, your first property is unlikely to be your forever home so it's a good idea to have resale in the back of your mind as well when choosing a home.

Location is important but you need also to think about the types of features you want in a home. For example, do you prefer a house or would you be happy with a unit? How many bedrooms and bathrooms would you like? Do you need off-street parking?

Make time to think about these factors. Of course, your budget may dictate your choices but it's a good idea to work out your must-haves and nice-to-haves and do up a wishlist (we all have to have a bit of fun in our lives).

When the time comes to look for a house, using sites such as realestate.com.au and domain.com.au is a no-brainer. Both sites also have apps that you can use to narrow down properties you want to check out. It's a good way to get an idea of what is out there.

You may also want to reach out to a few local real estate agents to give them an idea of what you're after. That way you may be one of the first people they contact when they get a new listing that fits what you're looking for.

Some home buyers may also opt to bring in the big guns and hire a buyer's agent to help them find a property. This can be an expensive way to go though. As a general guide fees may range from 1.5% to 3% of the purchase price. For more info on using a buyer's agent, see Chapter 17: I can get good advice.

You'll probably spend months going to open houses to inspect potential homes. They might start all blurring into one. You can make notes when you visit a property to remind you of any special features or things you liked or didn't like.

Some of the things you may want to pay attention to include:

- Are there any obvious mould or damp spots – pay particular attention to the bathroom and nearby rooms?

- Have you noticed any cracks anywhere?

- Are there any sagging spots on the ceiling?

- What is the light like? Is there lots of natural light?

- Turn on the taps to check that the water pressure is up to scratch.

- Is it relatively quiet or can you hear lots of noise?

5. Making the property yours

So, you have found THE home you want to make yours. Before you jump in and make an offer, stop and think. One of the decisions you'll need to make is how much you are willing to pay for it. Chances are by this stage you will have been keeping an eye on the market in the area so you'll have an idea what similar properties have been selling for.

Also check out sites such as propertyvalue.com.au and onthehouse.com.au as they provide estimates which can give you a ballpark figure. Of course, you also need to stick to your own budget as well.

It's important to get a conveyancer to look at the contract before you make an offer. They will be able to give you an idea of what is and isn't included and spot any special conditions you need to be aware of.

Getting the contract looked at is even more important if the property you are interested in is going to auction because there is no cooling-off period when you purchase at an auction.

There are two main ways property is sold in Australia – private treaty and auction. The approach you take to securing the house will vary based on the sale method. Let's take a look at both.

PRIVATE TREATY This means the property is advertised with a fixed price or at least a price range. There is usually room for negotiation here. Try to find out the seller's circumstances from the agent.

For example, if they have already bought a house or there is another reason they might want to sell quickly, you might be able to make a lower offer. You might also ask the agent if any offers have been made already and, if so, why they were rejected.

The way you play it will depend on how much demand you think there will be for the property. If you think there is likely to be a lot of competition, it might be best to make an offer close to your upper limit. You don't want to draw it out too long and have someone swoop in and nab the property while you're making lowball offers.

Even if it's a buyer's market, I wouldn't go in with an insulting offer – it pays to be fair. Some experts recommend you also set a deadline for the seller to accept any offer you make. There might be some back and forth and you might need to make several offers before one is accepted.

Once your offer is accepted you will have to sign the contract and pay a deposit. You may be able to ask for the offer to be 'conditional' on certain conditions being met, for example, subject to finance or a building and pest inspection.

There will also be a cooling-off period, which means you will be able to get out of the contract within that time frame should the need arise. Cooling-off periods vary from state to state and you will probably lose some of your deposit.

In NSW, for example, you have a five business-day cooling-off period after you exchange contracts. And if you withdraw during that time, you'll have to pay the seller 0.25% of the purchase price.

Make sure you understand the rules in your state or territory. Your conveyancer will be able to provide the relevant information.

AUCTION Auctions can be intense and if you want to avoid the stress of an auction you may want to try and secure the property before the big day by making a pre-auction offer. The risk of doing this is that if your offer is rejected you have shown your hand and what you are willing to pay.

If you are going to bid at auction, make sure you have everything sorted as there is no cooling-off period. That means having your finance approved, building and pest inspections done and the contract reviewed.

If you've never been to an auction before, it's a good idea to attend a few in the lead-up so you get a better idea of how things work and what to expect.

It's vital to know your limit – your absolute walkaway price – before you go to the auction and make sure you stick to it. Try not to let your emotions get the better of you on the day. It's a good idea to have someone with you during the auction to help keep you calm and on budget. You could also ask them to do the bidding for you.

Most experts recommend going in strong and that you project confidence. If you umm and ahh between each bid it could be construed as a sign of weakness by other bidders.

If the reserve price has been hit, the property is declared as being on the market. If you are the winning bidder, you'll need to sign the contract on the day and pay a 10% deposit. And remember there's no cooling-off period, so if for some reason you change your mind, you'll lose that 10%.

If the reserve price has not been met but you are the highest bidder when the property passes in then you'll be able to negotiate with the seller.

It's a good idea to take out building insurance as soon as the contracts are exchanged.

6. Settlement

Whether you buy the property through private treaty or at auction it's not officially yours until settlement. This is normally about six weeks after contracts are exchanged – unless you have negotiated something different.

ACTION PLAN

☐ *Set your goal deposit amount and start saving. Make sure you factor in the other upfront costs such as stamp duty and loan fees.*

☐ *Look for options that could help you boost your deposit such as family or government grants.*

☐ *Set your budget based on how much you have saved, how much you can borrow and the repayments you can afford.*

☐ *Get your finance sorted. Do some research on loans and find the right one for you.*

☐ *Get loan pre-approval so you know exactly how much you have to spend.*

☐ *Start looking for properties in areas you like and that tick your boxes.*

☐ *When you've found a home, do your research to work out how much you should pay.*

☐ *Get the contract reviewed by a solicitor or conveyancer.*

☐ *Make an offer or go to auction to secure the property.*

☐ *Get the necessary inspections done.*

☐ *Wait for settlement – and the property is yours!*

I CAN...

Pay for renos

If you ever want to liven up a dinner party, pull out a colour chart and ask the people around you for their opinions. Then sit back and watch as the conversation heats up, inevitably peppered by personal anecdotes about home renovations.

Australia is a nation of dedicated doer-uppers. And if the number of reality TV renovation shows isn't enough to convince you, the conga line of cars snaking around the car park of your local hardware store each Saturday morning should be.

And while those renovation reality shows focus on the latest designs, fittings and features, scant attention is paid to the nuts and bolts of how to pay for it all.

You can make home renovations a reality. But knowing how you'll pay for it all should be at the top of your list during the planning process.

It's easy to underestimate the costs involved – or worst-case scenario, run out of money midway through a project. When that happens, a dream bathroom can end up being a port-a-loo in the backyard until you've conjured up enough cash to complete the job.

There are lots of choices to be made when it comes to renovations, and the first one can be whether to stay put and renovate or move.

Renovate or relocate?

Sprucing up your place doesn't have to involve a big outlay. A fresh coat of paint or new floor coverings can work wonders on a small budget. At the other end of the scale, major renovations don't come cheap.

If you have a big project in mind, it's worth crunching the numbers to know if you're better off relocating rather than renovating. Sure, it may mean having to pay a real estate agent to sell the property and you'll have to fork out stamp duty to buy a house but it still might be the most cost-effective option.

Let's say, for instance, that Brisbane-based Sarah owns a $500,000 home. She loves the location but the kitchen and bathroom are in poor condition. Sarah is tossing up whether to upgrade the kitchen and bathroom, or step up to a $650,000 home where the hard work has already been done.

As Table 1 shows, upgrading to a new home could leave Sarah $33,400 out of pocket.

How does this compare to renovating? To estimate the cost of a new bathroom and kitchen, I used the latest Archicentre Australia Cost Guide, which is a handy reference for renovators, and is free to download from archicentreaustralia.com.au.

The results, in Table 2, show that Sarah could potentially put in a new bathroom for as little as $12,000, and renovate the kitchen for an extra $15,000. That's a total of $27,000 – $6,400 less than selling and buying a new place.

This assumes a basic renovation. As the Archicentre estimates show, Sarah could spend as much as $70,000 on her new kitchen/bathroom combo, potentially more.

These numbers highlight the importance of weighing up renovations with your heart and your head. If you're keen on a change of scenery, a move can be revitalising. If you love where you live, it may be worth staying and fixing up the place. Just be sure to take off the rose-coloured glasses before you start ripping up carpets or knocking down walls.

Renovations can be messy, disruptive and inconvenient. If the thought of sharing your home with a team of tradies – potentially for weeks or even months – gives you the cold shivers, it may be less stressful just to move.

TABLE 1 COST OF SELLING AND BUYING – QLD[1]

Real estate agent fees (2.8%, negotiable)	$14,000
Stamp duty on new property	$15,100
Conveyancing fees on sale and purchase	$2,400
Pre-purchase building and pest inspections	$500
Mortgage transfer documents	$400
Removalist fees	$1,000
Total moving costs	$33,400

[1]Based on sale of $500,000 home and purchase of $650,000 home.

TABLE 2 RENOVATION COSTS

	MINIMUM COST	MAXIMUM COST
Bathroom	$12,000	$27,000
Kitchen	$15,000	$43,000
Total renovation cost for both rooms	$27,000	$70,000

Source: 2019 Archicentre Australia Cost Guide

Beware the risk of overcapitalising

Be mindful of the risk of overcapitalising. That's when the cost of your renovations outweighs the value they add to the place.

Some improvements are classic culprits for overcapitalising, like swimming pools, which don't appeal to everyone because of the ongoing maintenance required. Other renovations, such as rewiring, may not add significant value simply because they're not obvious.

If in doubt, talk to a couple of local real estate agents for an idea of whether your planned project will deliver a decent uptick in your home's value.

RENOVATION MISTAKES TO AVOID

To ensure your reno goes as smoothly as possible it pays to be aware of the types of things that could end up costing you.

ACTING TOO QUICKLY

Most experts recommend living in a house for a year before deciding what work needs to be done.

OVERCAPITALISING

When the cost of the renovations outweighs the value they add.

UNDERESTIMATING THE COSTS

It's a good idea to add a 15%-20% buffer to what you think a project will cost.

CHASING CURRENT TRENDS

This could make the property harder to sell down the track.

NOT GETTING THE RIGHT APPROVALS

Renovating without the necessary permits can land you in trouble.

MOVING THE PLUMBING

Keeping the layout the same will save you money.

CHOOSING THE WRONG TRADESPERSON

Don't just go for the lowest bid and make sure you check references.

SKIMPING ON QUALITY

As they say, "buy well, buy once." Quality materials are more likely to last the distance.

CHANGING YOUR MIND

Making too many changes after the process has begun can cost you.

Set a reno budget

Drafting a renovation budget is a must-do. It shows what you'll be up for in costs, how much you need to outlay at different stages of the job, and it gives you a clear picture of what is – and isn't – affordable. This lets you scale your plans up or down in line with your finances.

To draw up a budget, compare prices of fittings and fixtures, gather quotes from builders, preferably at least three (always check that any tradies you deal with are licensed!), and, importantly, talk with your builder to be sure you're both on the same page when it comes to details like the type of cornice you want, which can impact the cost.

Importantly, add some wiggle room. Whether it's the Italian glass light fittings that get damaged in transit, or your builder discovering the floor isn't level halfway through the project, renovations have a habit of going over budget. Allowing for the unexpected can help you assess if you can afford to complete the project even if things don't go according to plan.

Also check whether your renovations need council approval. This is likely to be the case if you're making structural changes or adding to your home's footprint. Lodging plans with the council can bring a whole new set of fees but without council sign-off you could find it hard to sell your home later on.

Use a spreadsheet to draw up and monitor your budget, or download a budgeting app like Budget My Reno to keep track of the cost.

Develop a savings plan

Armed with a renovation budget, it's time to work out how to pay for your project. A Houzz survey found three out of four renovations are funded from personal savings, and while growing a pool of 'reno money' will take time, it can be done if you follow a dedicated savings plan.

The trick is to be realistic about how much you can save each month. Looking at Table 3 on page 110, for instance, if you have a project budget of $10,000, you'll need to save about $827 each month to reach $10,000 within 12 months. If you can wait, it's a lot easier to save $410 each month over two years to reach the same target. Plenty of online calculators can show how much you need to squirrel away each payday to accumulate funds for your project.

Play around with the numbers to decide what's achievable. Then put your savings on auto-pilot by setting up a regular funds transfer out of your everyday account and into a dedicated savings account.

TABLE 3 **MONTHLY SAVINGS NEEDED TO MEET RENOVATION COSTS**

Renovation cost	$10,000	$15,000	$20,000
Saving over a 12-month period	$827	$1,240	$1,653
Saving over a 2-year period	$410	$615	$820

Source: MoneySmart savings calculator. Assumes interest rate of 1.5%.

Put your home loan to work to pay for renovations

If the kids are complaining about sharing a bedroom, or there isn't enough room to swing a cat in your kitchen, let alone cook a Sunday roast, chances are that you'd like to get started on your renovations sooner rather than later. If that sounds like you, your home loan can be a source of low-interest finance, and there are several options to fund the project.

TAPPING INTO REDRAW OR OFFSET SAVINGS If you've been paying a bit extra off your home loan each month, it may be possible to claw back those payments through redraw. The beauty of this is that you have the freedom to withdraw only as much as you need, when you need it, leaving the remaining extra payments to reduce the loan balance and lower the overall interest cost.

It's the same story with cash in an offset account. However, pulling money out of your loan – be it through redraw or dipping into a linked offset account – is not a cost-free option. It will impact the long-term interest paid on the loan. Let's say the balance of your mortgage is $350,000. By pulling out $10,000 for renovations from redraw, you push the balance back up to $360,000. Even at an interest rate of just

3%, this could add as much as $4,200 to your total interest bill. This figure assumes you're at the start of a 25-year loan but regardless of the term remaining, ramping up the value of your home loan will come with an additional cost. The solution to keeping the additional interest bill to a minimum is to get back into the habit of making extra loan repayments or funnel cash into your offset account once the renovations are complete.

Quick tip – if you are planning to rely on redraw, check if limits apply to the number of redraws you can make annually. Watch for fees, too. Most lenders offer fee-free redraw, though some still charge up to $50 per withdrawal.

LOAN TOP-UP If you're thinking of major improvements, it may be possible to add the funds you need onto your existing mortgage with a home loan 'top-up'. The clincher can be whether you have sufficient home equity.

35%

OF RENOVATORS SAID THEIR BIGGEST CHALLENGE WAS FINDING THE RIGHT SERVICE PROVIDERS, ACCORDING TO A HOUZZ SURVEY.

Home equity is the difference between the value of your place and the balance owing on your mortgage. If your home is worth $700,000, and there is $300,000 owing on your loan, you have equity of $400,000. It's unlikely you'll be able to extend the loan by the full $400,000: lenders like to see a buffer of around 20% equity. But you may be able to borrow an additional $260,000. This would take the loan up to $560,000, which is 80% of your property's value, still leaving you with home equity of 20%.

In practice, how much you can borrow through a top-up also depends on your income. Banks want to be sure you can comfortably manage the repayments on a bigger loan. Plus, you'll need a squeaky-clean track record of making repayments on time. If you tick both boxes, check the fees that you'll pay. Some banks charge $400 for a loan increase.

Part of the appeal of a top-up is that your loan term generally stays the same. Be aware, though, that if your newly topped-up loan comes close to 80% of the property's value, the bank may shy away from handing over any further money. This reinforces the need to get your budget right from the beginning.

HOME LOAN REFINANCE Any time you're thinking of adding a decent chunk of money onto an existing home loan, it's worth taking a look to see if you could get a better deal by switching to a new lender. This is a process known as 'refinancing'. It may sound like a hassle, and it does involve some paperwork, but lenders often reserve their lowest rates for new customers. Switching loans could see you score the funds you need plus save with a lower rate.

We all love the idea of scoring a lower home loan rate, but there are traps with refinancing. If you want to borrow more than 80% of your home's value, you will be asked to pay lenders mortgage insurance (LMI) – even if you already paid LMI when you first bought the place. That's because LMI isn't transferrable between lenders, and as the cost can run into thousands of dollars, you need to stick below the 80% benchmark for refinancing to stack up financially.

Refinancing will also bring a new set of fees and charges. You could be looking at:

• A discharge fee on your old loan	$300-400
• An upfront fee on the new loan	$300-400
• State government mortgage registration/discharge fees	$300
Total fees	**$900-$1,100**

A decent rate saving should compensate for these fees, so shop around between lenders or partner with a mortgage broker to find the best rate for your ideal loan.

The biggest pitfall of refinancing is, potentially, that your new loan will automatically come with a 25- or 30-year term. It doesn't matter if you only had 15 or so years left on your old loan, you could find yourself back on the treadmill of a lengthy loan term. The solution is to negotiate with the new lender for a shorter term. Whether or not you get a thumbs-up depends on your income. The shorter the term, the higher your monthly repayments will be, and all lenders want to be certain you can manage the repayments for your preferred term.

CONSTRUCTION LOAN If you're looking at a seriously big project, construction loans can have a lot going for them. Unlike a loan top-up or refinance, the amount you can borrow is often based on your home's projected value after the renovations have been completed. This could mean access to a bigger pool of cash. That said, you will usually need to stump up a deposit, typically between 5% and 20% of the project cost.

Construction loans work a bit differently to regular mortgages. Instead of a lump sum of cash, the loan is drip-fed to you through a series of progress payments that coincide with various stages of the project. You only pay interest on the money drawn down and, during construction, loan payments are usually interest-only, leaving you with more disposable cash. When the project is completed, the loan reverts to principal-plus-interest payments.

In order to plan for progress payments, your bank may ask for a fixed-price contract that shows the total cost of the project. This can be a sticking point with your builder, who could push for a 'cost plus' contract, which will see you, the homeowner, wearing any unexpected hikes in the price of building materials.

The real clincher can be the cost. Construction loans usually charge a higher rate than traditional mortgages, and a fee of around $75 can apply to each progress payment. The bank may also ask you to take out various insurances including home warranty insurance that covers you if the builder goes bust, and public liability insurance so that you're protected if a slab of timber lands on next door's cat, and your neighbour decides to sue for damages.

It also pays to be absolutely sure about the renovations you're signing up for. If the contract price changes midway through the project

113

IF YOU ARE HIRING A
BUILDER FOR RENOVATION
WORK THEN CHANCES ARE
THAT THEY WILL ASK YOU
FOR A DEPOSIT. DEPENDING
ON WHERE YOU LIVE THERE
MAY BE LIMITS ON HOW
MUCH YOU HAVE TO PAY. IN
VICTORIA, FOR EXAMPLE,
BY LAW, YOUR DEPOSIT FOR
BUILDING WORK CAN BE NO
MORE THAN 10%, IF THE
TOTAL CONTRACT PRICE
IS LESS THAN $20,000
AND 5% IF IT'S $20,000
OR MORE. YOU CAN THEN
ARRANGE TO PAY FOR THE
REMAINDER IN STAGES BUT
DON'T HAND OVER ANY
MONEY UNTIL THE AGREED
WORK FOR EACH STAGE
IS COMPLETED.

– something that can happen when homeowners alter the original plans – the lender may want to reassess the loan all over again, and this can lead to delays. If any changes are minor, it may be quicker and easier to cover the cost out of your own pocket.

Construction loans are more complex than normal loans – more so if you already have a home loan in place, and want to use a construction loan from a different lender.

It can be done but, for my money, I'd speak with a decent mortgage broker to be sure you have the right loan structure in place.

The main takeaway is that, yes, you can pay for renovations. But just as you'll spend time researching and selecting the right materials and designs, it's also important to plan the best way to pay for your renos.

With the numbers sorted, you can focus on how to turn your place into a dream home, knowing you can comfortably pay for it all.

ACTION PLAN

☐ *Do your homework. Think about what features you want in your renovated home. Magazines and the internet can be a great source of inspiration.*

☐ *Weigh up whether renovating your existing house or buying a new house makes more sense for you.*

☐ *Start working on your renovation budget. Shop around to get an idea of the costs of fixtures and fittings you like and get at least three quotes from builders.*

☐ *Add a buffer to your reno budget to allow for any surprises that may arise through the process.*

☐ *Check whether your renovations need council approval and what is involved.*

☐ *Start saving money towards your renovation project.*

☐ *Explore the various financing options that may be available to work out what would work best for you.*

☐ *Make sure your builder and any tradies you use are registered and check out any reviews.*

They say if you want something, you have to put it out into the universe first. So, what do you want? Put it out there, write it down, scream it out but don't forget you still need to get the ball rolling.

In this section, you'll learn how to do just that. Invest with just $100, pick your own shares, choose your own ETFs, buy an investment property and retire on a healthy $50,000 a year. Not bad. Of course you should never say no to some expert help – and I have a section just on that!

PART IV

THINK RICH BE RICH

—

I CAN...

Invest with just $100 a week

Having money in a savings account always makes sense. It gives you access to emergency cash and your money is very safe. But that security can work against you. The returns on cash are very low, so it's not a way to make your money grow. And that's what investing is all about.

The thing about investing is that it's easy to assume you need to be wealthy to get started. A sharemarket survey by the ASX revealed that plenty of people feel this way. The study found that 30% of Australians who don't invest think it takes upwards of $2,000-$5,000 to start investing. One in four estimated that you need at least $10,000 to begin investing. Nothing could be further from the truth. In fact, it works the other way around. You build wealth by investing. What's more, you can be a successful investor with just $100 a week.

Compounding returns do the heavy lifting

What's so exciting about investing is that even small amounts can make a big difference to your wealth over time. And it's all thanks to the magic of compounding returns.

Compounding happens when you re-invest returns, so that you start to earn money on your initial investment plus previous returns. It can be a very powerful force, and with the benefit of compounding under your belt, your investments can grow exponentially over time.

To see how impressive the effects of compounding can be, let's say that from age 20, Olivia tucks $100 into an investment, earning 6.5% annually. Sure, it's a very small sum, but she backs it up by adding $100 to the same investment every week.

Graph 1 shows what can happen with Olivia's investment over time. The curved line is where all the action is – this is the total value of Olivia's investment. The lighter blue line shows how much money Olivia has added out of her own pocket: remember that's just $100 weekly.

For the first few years, Olivia's investment hums along, growing mainly through her $100 weekly contribution. But she reaches a point where compounding kicks in, and from there her wealth skyrockets as the returns on her investments start to make up an increasingly large proportion of the value of her investment.

As the graph shows, after 10 years, Olivia will have contributed $48,000 of her own money – but her investment will be worth $67,726. After another 10 years, when Olivia hits the 20-year mark, she will have tipped in $96,000 – but her investment is worth more than double this, at $197,231. By the 30-year anniversary, Olivia will have contributed $144,000 to her investment, which is now worth $444,868 – over three times the value of her contributions.

This exponential increase in the value of Olivia's investment over time is all thanks to the power of compounding. To demonstrate just how powerful it can be over time, if Olivia's parents started the same hypothetical investment regime when Olivia was born – and she later took it over as an adult – by age 50 Olivia's investment could be worth a cool $1.823 million, seven times the value of the $240,000 that has been chipped in over the previous five decades.

Okay, you probably don't want to wait 50 years to become a millionaire like Olivia. But as the graph confirms, it can take time for compounding to work its magic. The sooner you start, the sooner compounding can begin to do the heavy lifting and grow your wealth for you.

If Olivia can build a $1.8 million investment with just $100 a week, you can too. Let's take a look at the options for investing, when you want to start small.

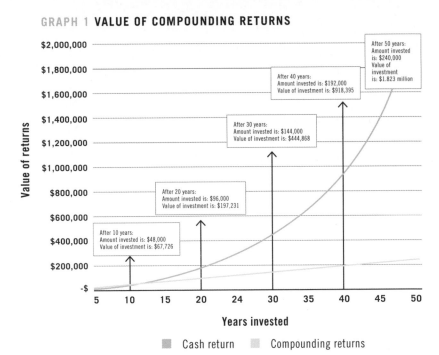

GRAPH 1 **VALUE OF COMPOUNDING RETURNS**

After 50 years:
Amount invested
is: $240,000
Value of
investment
is: $1.823 million

After 40 years:
Amount invested is: $192,000
Value of investment is: $918,395

After 30 years:
Amount invested is: $144,000
Value of investment is: $444,868

After 20 years:
Amount invested is: $96,000
Value of investment is: $197,231

After 10 years:
Amount invested is: $48,000
Value of investment is: $67,726

Value of returns

Years invested

Cash return   Compounding returns

Source: InvestSMART. Assumes: $100 invested each week for 50 years.
Return of 6.5% annually.

Micro-investing apps

When you don't have a lot to invest, micro-investing apps can make it easy. They work like electronic piggy banks, letting you invest very small sums in the sharemarket, the property market, even global asset markets. There are a number of micro-investing providers (or 'platforms') to choose from, so let's look at the more established options to understand what's involved.

RAIZ

Formerly known as Acorns, Raiz lets you grow your investments through lump sum deposits, regular deposits or by rounding up the loose change on purchases made with a linked credit or debit card. There is no minimum amount needed to open a Raiz account, but your money will only be invested once your Raiz account reaches $5.

Raiz offers a menu of seven ready-made portfolios. They range from conservative (least risky) to aggressive (most risky) as well as a sustainable investing option, and one portfolio that offers small exposure to Bitcoin. The common thread is that these portfolios are mainly comprised of various blends of exchange traded funds (ETFs) listed on the Australian Securities Exchange. I look more closely at ETFs in Chapter 13, but as a guide, they are very low-cost investments that invest in shares (both Australian and international) as well as other assets like property and government bonds.

Raiz is very much pitched at investors who are just starting out. In early 2020, for instance, the average account balance was $1,813.

The cost: Most Raiz portfolios charge a flat fee of $2.50 per month, which adds up to $30 annually. Once your investment grows to $10,000, you'll pay fees of 0.275% annually.

FIRSTSTEP

FirstStep works in much the same way as Raiz, although only $1 is needed to open a FirstStep account. A point of difference is that FirstStep lets you set personal 'rules' for investing based on your spending habits. For example, you may set a rule of automatically investing $10 every time you order Uber Eats.

FirstStep offers a choice of three core portfolio options – defensive, balanced and growth, which are made up of three ETFs managed by Vanguard, which is one of the most established ETF providers globally. From here, you can add investment themes like technology, health or ethical investments – again made up of exposure to various ETFs.

The cost: Expect to pay $1.25 per month ($15 annually) for accounts under $5,500, or $1.95 per month if you set up a regular direct debit from your everyday account into FirstStep. Once your account balance tops $5,500, the fee rises to 0.275% annually.

The verdict: Raiz and FirstStep aren't the only micro-investing apps, but the benefit of both these apps is the ability to start small and add to your portfolio over time.

A key issue to be aware of is that you do not directly own the underlying assets. What you are doing is investing in a fund managed by either Raiz or FirstStep, which pools your money with that of other investors, then spreads the money chiefly across various ETFs (in some cases with a smattering of other investments). It is important to know what you're signing up for because ETFs charge their own fees.

In the case of Raiz, the ETF fees range from 0.196% to 0.418% annually, and this comes on top of the fees charged directly by Raiz. With FirstStep, the underlying ETF fees vary between 0.15% to 0.5% annually.

The direct fees charged by these micro-investing apps are small in dollar terms. However, as an investor you need to look at fees as a percentage of your investment. This is important for two reasons. First, it lets you make an apples-for-apples comparison of the cost of different micro-investing platforms. Second, it shows how much your investment needs to earn so that you can pocket a decent after-fees return.

Here's an example. Let's say you have $500 invested with Raiz. The annual fee of $30 works out to 6% of your portfolio. In the background, though, you're also paying ETF fees, which as we've noted, can go as high as 0.418%. That means your investment may need to earn a return of at least 6.418% (depending on your choice of portfolio) just to break even.

With FirstStep, the annual fees of $15 add up to 3% of a $500 investment. On top of that you could be paying ETF fees of up to 0.5% (to keep things simple, we'll disregard the higher fee for a direct debit). So, your portfolio may need to earn returns of 3.5%, which is much more achievable, for you to break even. I'll take another look at the importance of fees later.

COMMSEC POCKET

CommSec Pocket is another micro-investing app but it works a bit differently in that you directly own the underlying investments. You can invest in a choice of seven ETFs with as little as $50 – that's one-tenth of the $500 first investment required for most securities, including ETFs, listed on the Australian sharemarket.

The ETFs lined up by CommSec Pocket run along various themes including 'Aussie top 20' and 'Emerging markets'. As you're not restricted to a pre-made portfolio, it's easy to mix and match your underlying ETFs. Reflecting this, your returns will hinge on the combination of ETFs you select.

The cost: Each time you trade using the app, you'll pay just $2, though trades worth over $1,000 cost 0.20% of the trade value. For example, a $1,500 trade will cost you $3. This is far less than you would pay for regular online broking, which can cost around $15-20 per trade.

As with Raiz and FirstStep, the ETFs you invest in charge their own underlying fees. The 'tech savvy' theme, for instance, is backed by the BetaShares NASDAQ 100 ETF, which charges a fee of 0.48%. These fees are low, although they are an added expense on top of brokerage.

There is a potential hidden cost with CommSec Pocket. You'll need to open a Commonwealth Bank transaction account to use CommSec Pocket, and the CommBank Everyday Account comes with a $4 monthly fee. This cost can be avoided if you deposit at least $2,000 into the account each month. But if you don't tick this box, one month's account fee of $4 can cost you the equivalent of two trades on CommSec Pocket.

The verdict: CommSec Pocket has a lot going for it if you're starting out small. The drawback is that you're limited to ETFs that you can buy into with just $50 – and these are not always what some pundits would regard as the market leaders.

As a guide, Vanguard is one of the biggest ETF providers globally, but it is not represented among the ETFs available through CommSec Pocket, and that may be because its ETFs don't always tick the box for trading below $50.

As always, it pays to look at CommSec Pocket's fees. They may be small but they can add up. If you were to invest $100 each week – a total of $5,200 in a year – you'd end up paying brokerage of $104 over a 12-month period. If you used a regular online broker charging, say, $15 per trade, you could make four trades of $1,300 each quarter, and end up paying $60 in brokerage, and still have the same amount invested at the end of a year.

BRICKX

What if you'd rather invest in property than ETFs? There's a micro-investing solution for that too.

BrickX is a platform that lets you buy a stake in a selection of 19 different rental properties with as little as $50. The value of each property is divided into 10,000 'Bricks', so if you want to invest in a property valued at $350,000, each Brick would cost $35. You can choose which property you'd like to invest in or, alternatively, invest $50 monthly and have your money automatically spread across a variety of properties.

Once you've invested, you can expect to receive a monthly share of the property's net rent (that's rental income less expenses like maintenance and insurance) in line with the number of Bricks you hold. If you own 5% of Bricks in a property, you'll receive 5% of the net rent.

The net rental yields for each property are listed on the BrickX website. In mid-2020, they typically ranged from around 1.5% to about 2.5%. This may not sound like much, but bear in mind this is rent left over after a range of costs, including property management fees, have been paid out. By the way, these costs are all taken care of on your behalf: you don't need to worry about a tenant phoning on a Sunday afternoon to let you know the roof is leaking.

You can cash in your Bricks by offering them for sale on the BrickX site but they can only be sold to other BrickX subscribers. This may mean you might not be able to sell them quickly.

The cost: There are no ongoing fees with BrickX. Instead, you pay a 0.5% transaction fee each time you buy or sell a Brick. Let's say you invest in a new $100 Brick each week. Over the space of a year, you could have accumulated around $5,200 in Bricks, with transaction fees of $26. If you sell all the Bricks at the end of the year, you could be up for another $26 in fees.

The verdict: BrickX offers a chance to indirectly invest in residential property for a tiny fraction of what it would cost to buy a place directly. And you benefit from hassle-free rent returns plus the potential for capital gains as the property grows in value over time.

However, there can be a question mark over what those capital gains will be. Each property's market value is displayed on the site, and you're free to ask whatever price you like for a Brick when you decide it's time to bail out. The catch is that Bricks can only be sold to other BrickX subscribers, and this could mean you're facing a smaller pool of buyers than if you were selling the property on the open market. In mid-2020, for instance, Bricks in a number of properties were selling for around 10% below market valuation. There can be a variety of reasons for this but it's a reminder that capital gains are not guaranteed when you invest in property, especially if you don't hold onto your investment for the long term (that's at least five years), and this downside can be accentuated when you have a limited pool of buyers.

PEER TO PEER INVESTING

The idea behind peer to peer (P2P) or 'marketplace' lending is that it lets ordinary Aussies lend to people looking for a loan, and earn a return in much the same way that banks do. You're not handing your cash directly over to a borrower. Instead, what typically happens is that you invest in a managed fund that provides finance for personal lending. That's not a bad idea, especially if you only have a small sum to invest, as it means your money is spread across a number of borrowers, which helps to reduce the risk of non-payment by any particular borrower.

The drawback is that unless you have a decent chunk of cash to invest (in some cases $100,000 or more), P2P lending is really only available through one provider – Plenti (formerly known as RateSetter).

Plenti lets you start investing with as little as $10. You choose the lending market that suits you, each of which comes with different potential interest rates. It may seem like a no-brainer to invest in higher-rate loans, but it can take longer to find suitable borrowers willing to pay a more expensive rate and you only earn a return when your money is being loaned out.

From there, you can opt to receive regular payments as borrowers pay down their loans, or automatically reinvest the returns.

The cost: Plenti charges a fee of 10% of the gross interest earned.

The verdict: P2P investing has the potential to deliver a higher return than cash held in a bank account. According to Plenti, annual returns of 6% are possible.

But this type of lending does come with risks. Plenti is not a bank, so as an investor your money isn't protected by the government guarantee on funds that applies to traditional savings accounts and term deposits. Plenti says it manages this risk by checking the credit worthiness of borrowers, and by having a 'provision fund' that borrowers contribute to, which covers possible loan defaults. That said, Plenti makes it clear that this is not a guarantee that you'll get your money back if a borrower heads off into the sunset leaving their loan unpaid.

A quick point to note: Plenti offers terms ranging from one month through to seven years. However, the one-month deposit is a 'rolling' facility. Put simply, your money may be invested in loans with a longer term that one month, so there is a possibility that your money may also need to stay invested for longer. It's something to be aware of if you really want to cash out your investment within a month.

Why fees are so important when you're starting out small

No matter how you choose to invest, whether it's through small change on purchases or regular payments, the thing to watch out for is fees. Unlike returns, which will almost certainly vary from year to year – including falling into negative territory (meaning you cop a loss) – your fees are set in stone. Just as compounding returns can grow the value of your wealth over time, fees can easily eat into your investments.

The bottom line is to keep an eye on fees – not just the dollar value, but what they work out to as a percentage of the money you have invested.

ROBO ADVICE: WHEN YOU'RE READY TO UPGRADE

Micro-investing can be an easy way to launch into investing when you don't have much cash to get started.

Once you've built up some funds it can work out cheaper to invest directly, especially when it comes to ETFs. But if you like the idea of effortless investing, where someone else manages your portfolio at very low cost, another option can be robo advice or automated online investing.

Robo advice typically centres on complex computer algorithms that work out the best way for you to invest, and from there automatically rebalance your portfolio so that your investments stay relevant to your needs over time. You can read more about robo advice and how it works in Chapter 17: I can find good advice.

But here's the thing. You may not need robo advice. Successful investing is not hard. Sure, it does rely on sticking to some basic rules (and maybe a healthy dose of commonsense), however, as we'll see in the chapters that follow, once you've accumulated just a small amount of capital, a whole world of investing can open up for you.

FAST FACT

OVER A 30-YEAR PERIOD, PAYING FEES OF 2% RATHER THAN 1% CAN REDUCE THE VALUE OF YOUR FINAL BALANCE BY UP TO 20% (FOR EXAMPLE, REDUCING IT FROM $100,000 TO $80,000).

ACTION PLAN

☐ *Think about what you would like to invest in and look at the platforms that give you that option.*

☐ *Take a closer look at the available investment options and how they have performed over the long term.*

☐ *Find out all the fees that may be charged. For example, are there any underlying fees such as an ETF management fee?*

☐ *Develop an understanding of how it works and make sure it suits your needs.*

☐ *Find out what is involved if you want to sell your investment.*

I CAN...

Pick my own shares

Picture this. You buy into a business, earn a slice of the profits and have a stake in the growth of the company over time – all without having to lift a finger to run the enterprise. It's not a bad deal, and that's exactly what you get by investing in shares. You don't have to be an investment guru to get started, and as long as you follow some basic rules, it can be an effortless way to grow your wealth.

This explains why shares are one of our most popular investments. One in three Australians directly owns shares, according to the ASX Investor Study 2017, and you can too. But before you even start choosing shares you need to understand how they work.

Get to know how shares work

Investing in shares can seem complex, and yes, there's a whole lot of jargon that goes hand-in-hand with sharemarkets. But the basics of shares are very straightforward.

When you invest in shares, you are buying a small slice of ownership in a company listed on the Australian Securities Exchange (ASX). The sharemarket is broken into various sectors including energy, financial, utilities, consumer staples and healthcare.

As a shareholder you are a part owner of a very big business. It doesn't matter whether the company is Telstra, Qantas, one of the mining giants like BHP or any one of the 2,000 other companies listed on the ASX, as a shareholder you own part of the business – and that's pretty exciting.

As a part owner, you have the right to attend the company's annual general meeting and have your say in how the business should be run. It's an option, but most shareholders are happy to sit back and leave the daily grind to the Board of Directors.

The real appeal of shares lies in the opportunity to earn income without any personal effort. And unlike a rental property, once you've paid for shares, you won't be asked to contribute extra cash to keep the business going. Even better, the returns on shares can be very lightly taxed.

Sounds too good to be true? It's not. But just as there are upsides to shares, there are also pitfalls you need to know about.

How shares can make money

As a shareholder, you have the potential to earn two types of income – dividends and capital gains. They are quite different, and it's worth understanding what's involved with each.

Each year, when a company makes a profit (assuming it makes a profit), all or part of this money can be paid out to shareholders as 'dividends'.

Unlike interest on a savings account, there are no guarantees about dividends. It is up to the Board of Directors to decide whether the company will pay a return to shareholders at all. During the Covid-19 pandemic, for instance, a number of companies decided to hold onto their cash rather than pay a dividend. To be fair, these were exceptional circumstances, and depending on the company you invest in, you can normally expect to receive a dividend payment once or twice a year.

How much you'll receive will depend on how many shares you own. Even better, dividends can be tax-friendly, thanks to our system of 'franking credits'. This simply means that at tax time you'll be credited for any tax the company paid on the profits that the dividends were distributed from. As the company tax rate is 30%, if you are a high-income earner with a personal tax rate of 45% (excluding the Medicare Levy), you may only pay 15% tax on your dividend income. If you're a low-income earner you could even receive a refund for the tax paid by the company.

DIVIDENDS: WHAT YOU SHOULD KNOW

One of the ways you can make money from shares is through dividends, which are essentially a portion of the company's profits paid to shareholders.

WHAT IS IT?

A payment from a company to its shareholders.

HOW OFTEN IS IT PAID?

Most companies pay dividends twice a year – usually there is an 'interim' dividend and a 'final' dividend.

FOR EXAMPLE

Happy Saver Limited pays a dividend of 10¢ per share. If you own 1,000 shares you will be paid $100.

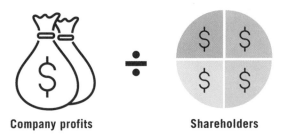

Company profits   **Shareholders**

Need to know

+ Not all companies pay dividends.

+ Find out if they are fully franked.

+ You can choose to have the dividends paid as cash or reinvest them to buy additional shares in the company.

CAPITAL GAINS – PROFIT FROM A RISE IN SHARE VALUES

The second way to make money on shares is through capital gains. This can happen when your shares rise in value over time. Happily, capital gains can also be lightly taxed.

Let's say, for instance, that you buy 1,000 shares in Happy Saver Limited paying $10 per share. That makes your investment worth $10,000. Business booms for Happy Saver Limited, and two years later the shares are worth $15, so your investment is now valued at $15,000. How good is that? You've made a capital gain of $5,000 with absolutely no effort.

One of the great things about shares is that no matter how much they rise in value, the capital gains are only taxed when you sell them. And if you hold onto your shares for over 12 months, the ATO lets you claim a 50% discount on the profits you make. So, if you sold those Happy Saver Limited shares when they reached $15 after two years, you'd only pay tax on $2,500 not the full profit of $5,000.

BE PREPARED FOR UPS AND DOWNS AND THINK LONG TERM

By now you're probably beginning to see the appeal of shares. Is there a catch? Well, yes. Just like dividends, there are no guarantees that your shares will rise in value. There is always the possibility that the company you invest in turns out to be a dud, and the shares fall in value over time, meaning you make a capital loss. That's definitely not so much fun. One of the best ways to protect yourself against this is by choosing your shares with care to be confident the company has decent growth prospects.

I'll look at how to pick shares shortly, but even if you tick all the boxes, and invest in well-managed companies, there can be times when the sharemarket takes a dive. The start of the coronavirus pandemic, for instance, saw global sharemarkets tank – almost overnight, in early 2020. Even the biggest companies experienced falling share values.

Thankfully, these sorts of market drops don't happen often, but it is something you need to be aware of. It's not always obvious that a downturn is coming, and when share values start to fall it can be easy to panic and sell out your shares. It can take nerves of steel to sit tight during a downturn, however it's often your best strategy. Sharemarkets have always experienced highs and lows, for a whole variety of reasons. But history has shown that the market goes on to recover – often to bigger and better things, and the general trend over time is for values to head upwards.

That said, the possibility of a market downturn explains why shares are regarded as a long-term investment. By that, I mean you need to be prepared to hold onto your shares for at least five to seven years, preferably longer. This way you allow time for your investment to recover from any possible downswings. It can help to look at it this way. If you're currently aged 30, only invest money in shares that you don't expect to need until at least age 35, maybe 40. And be prepared to ride out any market downturns. Your future self will thank you for it.

Choosing your shares

This is where things get really exciting. With more than 2,000 shares listed on the ASX it can seem like a lottery choosing which ones to invest in. But it shouldn't be.

Always remember the golden rule that when you buy shares you are becoming a part owner in the business. Think of it this way. If a friend asked you to invest in her business, chances are you'd ask some serious questions like: How will it make money? Who's running the show? What sort of competition does the business face? It's no different when it comes to investing in listed companies. You need to ask the same questions to check whether the business has decent growth prospects.

A big advantage of listed companies is that you have a lot more tools at your disposal to know whether you're picking a winner or tipping money into a dud. When you start out in shares, it can make sense to stick with the large companies. They are easier to research, and have a proven track record and an established business. The company's website will tell you plenty about what it does, or just Google the company name for any news being reported in the media. Then narrow down the choice by thinking about the following issues:

HOW DOES THE COMPANY MAKE MONEY?

You want to invest in a business that you understand. It just makes it easier to know what sort of risks the company (and your shares) could face. It's easy to grasp how a company like Woolworths makes money, and you don't have to be an expert to realise that no matter what sort of shape the economy is in, people need to buy groceries. It's a similar story with the big banks such as NAB, Westpac or CBA, or the major telcos such as Telstra.

There are other large companies with successful businesses that you may not be so familiar with. CSL, for example, is one of the largest collectors of blood serum in the world – a product that will always be in demand.

DOES THIS COMPANY HAVE A COMPETITIVE ADVANTAGE?

Some companies have an edge in the market by having a product that's hard for competitors to imitate. This gives the company a competitive advantage – good news for you as a shareholder.

In Australia, for instance, Transurban operates some of the nation's biggest toll roads such as the CityLink in Melbourne and Sydney's Cross City Tunnel. It's hard to see another company building competing toll roads any time soon, which can give companies like Transurban a distinct advantage in the market.

WHAT COULD IMPACT THE COMPANY IN THE FUTURE?

None of us has a crystal ball, but thinking about what could impact a company further down the track often calls for a bit of commonsense.

Technology can be a key cause of success – or failure – even among the most successful companies. Twenty years ago, camera company Kodak was a leading global brand. But it failed to tap into the digital boom, and in 2012 the company filed for bankruptcy. Fast forward to 2020, and so-called digital disrupters like Netflix, iTunes, Uber, and Amazon are all having a big impact on a variety of traditional industries.

Consider lifestyle changes, too. Our ageing society could drive demand for aged care services. Environmental concerns could see more consumers turn away from coal-fired power and embrace alternative energies like wind, biomass and solar power.

These issues may not impact a company immediately, but if you plan to hang onto your shares for the long term, which you should, it makes sense to look ahead.

A NUMBER TELLS A THOUSAND WORDS

There is another way to narrow down your choice of shares, and that's by putting some key figures under the microscope. Yes, it's a numbers game, but certain ratios can say plenty about a listed company.

Forget about dusting off your calculator; your broking platform will likely provide the main ratios for each company. If not, jump onto the ASX website, which displays the main ratios for each listed company. What matters is that you have an idea what the numbers mean.

45%

OF THOSE WHO BEGAN INVESTING IN THE 12 MONTHS TO JANUARY 2020 WERE WOMEN, ACCORDING TO AN ASX STUDY.

Market cap: 'Market capitalisation' isn't a ratio, but it's still a handy number. It shows the number of shares issued by the company multiplied by the shares' current market value. Think back to Happy Saver Limited – if the company issued 10 million shares and the shares were trading for $10 apiece, its market cap would be $100 million. That's a big sum for me and you – but not by ASX standards. Many of our biggest listed companies have a market cap measured in the billions of dollars. In fact, Happy Saver Limited would be regarded as a 'small cap' – or small listed company. Big companies are not necessarily better. Smaller companies can be more agile, but they tend to have fewer resources to weather the storms of market/economic downturns.

Annual dividend yield: This is one figure that should catch your eye, especially if regular dividend income is your main driver for investing in shares. The dividend yield lets you compare ongoing returns between different companies – as well as being a way to compare returns on shares to other investments like cash or property. To work out the dividend yield, divide the annual dividend per share by the share price. As a guide, if Happy Saver Limited paid an annual dividend of 50 cents per share, and its shares are trading at $10, the dividend yield would be 5.0% ($0.50 ÷ $10). What does this mean? Well, if you compare a 7.5% dividend yield to the returns you'd earn on cash, let's say 2%, it's easy to see that the dividend yield is a far better return.

Earnings per share (EPS): This shows the amount of profit earned for every ordinary share issued. You can work it out by dividing the company's net profit by the number of shares issued. What you're looking for is how the EPS changes over time. Ideally, the company will be steadily growing its EPS year after year.

Price earnings (PE) ratio: This is worked out by dividing the most recent share price by earnings per share. It's a favourite among investors as it's a way of measuring the earnings potential of a company. A very low PE ratio can mean the company is performing poorly especially in relation to its competitors. On the other hand, a high PE ratio can show a company has growth potential. You don't need to work out the PE ratio yourself. The ASX website displays the PE ratio for every listed company, with a side-by-side comparison of its main competitors.

Placing your first trade – you've got this!

Buying and selling shares on the ASX is called 'trading', and the minimum order size for your first trade in a company is $500. While you could technically get started with just $500, it won't allow you to diversify into other companies. Also, there's the brokerage fees that you need to factor in, too.

Before you begin trading, you'll need to choose an online broker. Trades can only be placed through an ASX-authorised broker – you can't buy shares directly from the company. Fortunately, there is no shortage of online brokers that make it quick, easy and inexpensive to trade shares.

Some online brokers such as CommSec and NabTrade are linked to our biggest banks. Others such as CMC Markets are independent. The common thread is very low rates of brokerage – often less than $20 per trade. That matters because the lower the brokerage, the more of your money goes towards your investment. So, for example, if the brokerage fee is $20 and you only invest $500, your stock would need to rise by at least 8%, or $40, for you to break even as you'll also pay brokerage to exit the trade. The bigger your investment, the less impact the brokerage fee has on your net returns.

When it comes to choosing your online broker, don't just go for the cheapest platform you can find. There's not a huge difference in cost between most online brokers, and it can be more important to feel comfortable with the way your broker's site is set up. The other thing to look for when you're checking out different broking sites is what exactly your money buys – especially the quality of sharemarket research you're able to access.

When you find a broker you're comfortable with, it's time to start trading. It's a really easy five-step process.

1. SET UP YOUR TRADING ACCOUNT

Set up a cash account linked to the trading account with your online broker. This account will store the money you need to pay for shares, and will be where any dividends are paid into. Your broking platform will guide you through the process of opening a linked account.

2. DEPOSIT FUNDS INTO YOUR LINKED ACCOUNT

When your cash account is up and running, transfer enough funds to pay for your first trade – remember this is a minimum of at least $500 plus the cost of brokerage.

3. PLACE YOUR FIRST BUY ORDER

Things are getting real now! After you've logged into your trading account, select the 'trading' option, and fill in the details of your trade. Quick tip – double-check that you enter the right 'ticker' code for the shares you want to buy. Each company listed on the ASX has its own ticker (or stock) code, but some are similar and a simple typo can lead to a big mistake. For instance, you may want to buy shares in resource company Rio Tinto (ticker code RIO) but if you mistakenly enter RIC as the stock code, you could end up buying a stake in Ridley Corporation, which makes food for livestock. Double-check your order. It's better to be safe than sorry.

Next, choose whether you want to buy or sell – your first trade will be a 'buy'. Enter the number of shares you'd like to invest in, or set a dollar limit for your trade.

4. CHOOSE THE TYPE OF ORDER YOU WANT TO PLACE

Your broking platform is likely to ask whether you want to make a 'market' order, which means you are comfortable paying whatever the share is currently trading for; or a 'limit' order, which lets you set the maximum price you're willing to pay. A market order is probably fine for your first trade.

5. DOUBLE-CHECK YOUR ORDER

Your broking platform will ask you to review your order. Use this opportunity to be sure you have entered the correct details. Then click to complete your trade, and hey presto, you're now a sharemarket investor.

Hold onto all paperwork for tax time.

FAST FACT

AUSTRALIAN SHARES PRODUCED A NEGATIVE RETURN IN ONLY FIVE YEARS FROM 1990 TO 2019, ACCORDING TO VANGUARD. THE BEST YEAR WAS 2007, WITH AUSTRALIAN SHARES RETURNING 30.3% IN THAT FINANCIAL YEAR WHILE THE WORST WAS 2009 WITH SHARES FALLING BY 22.1%.

ACTION PLAN

☐ *Start with companies that you know or industries or sectors that interest you.*

☐ *Keep an eye on financial news to work out what is happening in the economy that may affect the company or industry.*

☐ *Think about what you want from your investment – is it mainly income or capital growth?*

☐ *Pull together annual reports, investor presentations, company alerts and also Google news to see what is being said about the company you have chosen.*

☐ *Think about how the company is making money, what its competitors are doing and what factors could affect its future.*

☐ *Take a look at the financial information such as PE ratio, EPS and dividend yield.*

☐ *To spread your risk, you should aim to eventually have shares in the main sectors.*

I CAN...

Choose my own ETFs

Everybody loves a 'twofer'. You know, those special deals where you buy two for the price of one. Well, imagine a way to invest in dozens of different shares, all for a single upfront price. That's exactly what exchange traded funds (ETFs) are about. If you love a good deal, chances are you'll love the value, simplicity and diversity that ETFs can bring to your portfolio.

What are ETFs?

ETFs are a type of managed fund listed on the Australian Securities Exchange (ASX). There's nothing new about managed funds, they've been around for decades, and most Australians are familiar with the concept of managed funds through their superannuation.

As I mentioned in Chapter 11: I can invest with just $100 a week, managed funds work by pooling the cash of a large group of investors, then directing the money into specific investments as determined by the fund manager.

In this sense, all managed funds let investors enjoy far more diversity than most of us could achieve on our own. A single managed fund can provide exposure to multiple companies, entire industry sectors like technology or infrastructure, commodities such as gold and oil, and even hard-to-access investments such as international bond or equity markets.

The term 'exchange traded' points to one of the key differences between ETFs and the managed funds offered by some of our biggest financial institutions (also known as unlisted funds). ETFs are listed on the ASX, so they can be bought and sold just like shares, except that instead of becoming a shareholder in a company, you become a unitholder of the fund.

It's the investment style, however, that sets many ETFs apart from regular managed funds. Rather than using an 'active' strategy, where the fund manager analyses the market looking for the next winning investments, most ETFs follow a 'passive' approach. Also known as 'index' investing, this means ETFs aim to mirror the returns of a given market index. So, if an index rises 5% in a year, you'd expect the units in an ETF to climb in value by around 5%. The reverse also applies. If the index drops 5%, the ETF's units are likely to experience a similar decline in value.

There is no shortage of market indices to follow. Some ETFs, like the Vanguard Australian Shares Index Fund, aim to replicate the returns of the ASX 300 Index, which tracks the performance of Australia's top 300 listed companies. Others, such as the BetaShares NASDAQ 100 ETF, aim to track the NASDAQ 100 Index – an index that measures the returns of some of the world's biggest tech companies such as Apple, Amazon and Alphabet (which owns Google). Other ETFs focus on more obscure indices that track anything from the price of gold bullion to bank bills or corporate bonds. Long story short, if there's an index, it's a reasonable bet there's an ETF tracking it.

Why choose a passive approach?

At this stage you may be wondering why anyone would invest in a fund that only aims to mirror market returns. Why not go the extra distance and try to beat the index? After all, the whole point of investing is to make money.

The thing is that although the idea of beating the market is very attractive, doing so is considerably harder. A whole cocktail of ingredients come together to shape investment market returns. The state of the economy, changes to government legislation, investor sentiment, shifts in consumer behaviour, and the development of new technologies are just some of the factors that influence the performance of investment markets. In this complex environment, figuring out which investments will do well calls for a blend of good research, good timing – and in many cases, good luck. And even the experts don't get it right all the time.

As a guide to how hard it is for actively managed funds to outpace the market, over the five years to the end of 2019, just 19% of actively managed Australian share funds achieved above-market returns, according to the SPIVA (S&P Indices Versus Active) scorecard. Eight out of 10 failed to even match the overall market returns. The catch is that even the high achievers can find their winning streak is short-lived. I've come across research that tracked the results of the top-performing actively managed funds in 2015. It found that just 1.7% of these funds consistently beat market benchmarks in the following four years.

That's not to say that actively managed funds don't have a place in your portfolio – and as noted, your super is a good example of this type of investment. But this doesn't alter the reality that while actively managed funds can outpace the market in some years, very few do it year after year.

Low-cost investing

Another appealing fact about ETFs, and one that has put them on the investment map, is that they charge incredibly low fees.

All managed funds charge fees, that's how the fund manager makes money. With an actively managed fund, you can expect to pay annual fees of about 1% annually and, in some cases, more. But with an ETF it's possible to pay as little as 0.03% annually. To put that in perspective, if you invested $1,000, you'd pay just 30 cents in fees over the course of a year – to pay fees this low on an investment represents amazing value. And the lower the fees, the more of each year's returns end up in your pocket rather than the fund manager's.

It's the passive, index-based approach of ETFs that makes such low fees possible. Unlike actively managed funds that require teams of analysts to research markets and spot potential winners, ETFs cost very little to run. They typically hold a representative basket of investments in similar proportions to the index the fund is following. This demands less work and less research, and that means lower fees.

As an investor, you could in theory indulge in your own spot of DIY index investing by buying each of the shares that make up an index. It's possible, but with well over 2,000 shares listed on the ASX, you'd need a generous budget – and you'd rack up some very solid brokerage costs in the process. It all sounds like way too much work to me, especially when ETFs offer a simple, low-cost way to spread your money across multiple underlying investments.

Making money on ETFs

When you buy into an ETF you are investing indirectly in the fund's assets. In a share-based ETF, for instance, you don't own the shares yourself, but as a unitholder the returns on the fund's investments will flow through to you in the form of distributions. These can work in much the same way as dividends paid to shareholders, and are usually paid quarterly, half-yearly or annually. In this sense, some ETFs have the potential to be a source of regular income.

The second way to make money on ETFs is through an increase in the value of your units. Let's say that Paige purchased 100 units in the SPDR S&P Emerging Markets Fund in February 2016. Back then she would have paid around $15 per unit, giving her a total investment of $1,500. By August 2020, the same units were trading for $20, taking Paige's investment to $2,000, meaning she has made a capital gain of $500 – a return of about 33.33% over five years.

Of course, there are no guarantees with capital gains. You could make a capital loss if the value of your units falls, which can happen if the index that underpins the ETF experiences a downturn.

Getting started in ETFs

To begin investing in ETFs, you'll need to sign up with an online broker who does the buying and selling of ASX-listed securities on your behalf. I walk you through the process involved in placing a trade using an online broker on page 138, Chapter 12: I can pick my own shares.

As with shares, the minimum marketable parcel is $500, so you'll need at least this much plus the price of brokerage to get started with your first ETF trade.

Before you launch into ETFs, have a think about how often you want to add to your portfolio – either by growing your investment in a single ETF or by spreading your money across multiple ETFs, which will bring further diversity to your portfolio.

One issue to weigh up in this decision is the cost of your trades. The beauty of online brokerage is that it's very cheap at around $15-20 per trade, but making frequent trades will quickly see the cost add up. Make two trades a month at $15 each, for example, and over the course of a year you'll have forked out $360 in brokerage. Great for your broker. Not so good for you.

On the flipside, there's a strong argument for investing regularly. Sticking to a pattern of investing a set amount over fixed intervals – monthly, quarterly or every six months – is a strategy known as 'dollar cost averaging'. Take a look at the infographic on page 148 which demonstrates how it works.

Dollar cost averaging has several benefits including taking the emotion out of investing, and helping to reduce the impact of market highs and lows, so that you end up paying more of an average price for your ETF units over time. It's also a lot less hassle than trying to guess the 'right' time to buy into the market.

The downside of dollar cost averaging is that it can see your brokerage costs climb rapidly, especially if you opt for a more frequent pattern of investing such as monthly rather than quarterly.

The trick is to find the sweet spot between how often you tip money into ETFs while minimising brokerage. One way to save on brokerage is by following a pattern of putting a set amount of cash aside into an online saver account each week, then when you've accumulated, say $1,000, invest a lump sum as a single block into your preferred ETF.

LUMP SUM INVESTMENT VS REGULAR INVESTMENT PLAN (DOLLAR COST AVERAGING)

Making regular investments instead of a lump sum upfront can have its advantages. Here's a look at how it works.

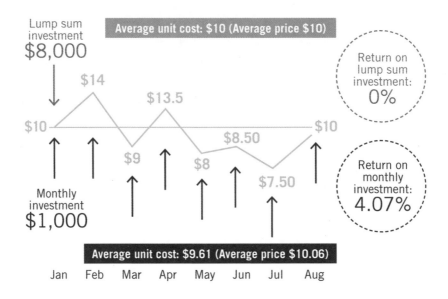

Lump sum investment
$8,000

Average unit cost: $10 (Average price $10)

$14

$13.5

$10

$8.50

$9

$8

$7.50

$10

Return on lump sum investment:
0%

Return on monthly investment:
4.07%

Monthly investment
$1,000

Average unit cost: $9.61 (Average price $10.06)

Jan Feb Mar Apr May Jun Jul Aug

Need to know

+ Let's say you have $8,000 to invest. You can choose to invest all at once, or invest $1,000 at the start of each month for eight months.

+ Investing a fixed dollar amount on a regular schedule averages out your buy-in price over the investment's lifetime.

+ By investing regularly you're buying more shares when prices are lower, fewer when prices are higher, which can bring down the average price.

+ By drip-feeding your money into the market you minimise the impact of short-term price movements on your investment.

Choosing your ETFs – what to weigh up

With an ever-expanding menu of ETFs to choose from, it's possible to build a truly diverse portfolio with very little outlay. You'll have your own ideas on which ETFs to invest in but there are some factors to weigh up.

FEES MATTER – BUT THEY'RE NOT ALL THAT MATTERS

Across the ETF market, the average fund fee is around 0.49%, although there can be big variations between funds, even among those that focus on the same underlying asset class.

There can be a variety of reasons for the difference in fees, including the cost structures of various funds, the fund size, and the technique used to replicate index returns.

Paying higher fees doesn't necessarily mean you're buying into a better fund, and it's certainly no indication of earning higher returns – especially in an index fund. Sure, fees matter but focus first on the ETFs that suit your goals. Don't buy into a fund simply because it seems cheap.

There's another cost that's not so well known and that is the buy/sell spread, also known as bid/ask spread. This is simply the difference between what a seller is asking for each of their units in an ETF and what a buyer is willing to pay.

The smaller the spread, the less you have to pay. Spreads can be an indication of liquidity and supply and demand; generally, popular stocks will have a lower spread and less-traded stocks will have a wider spread.

ARE YOU REALLY BUYING INTO AN INDEX FUND?

Not all funds listed on the ASX are index funds. Some are actively managed and can charge higher fees including, in some cases, an 'outperformance' fee, which kicks in if the fund achieves returns above a certain level.

The best way to pick index funds from listed managed funds is to visit the web page of the fund for details on its approach to investing.

DIVERSIFICATION

ETFs are undoubtedly a low-cost way to add instant diversity to your portfolio, but some ETFs are more diverse than others. This often depends on the index or benchmark an ETF is aiming to replicate.

Some ETFs, for example, follow sectors like the finance or resource industries. By their nature, these won't be as diversified as funds that track the broader sharemarket. Give some thought to how you can mix and match ETFs to achieve your ideal blend of diversification.

International ETFs: to hedge or not to hedge?

ETFs can make it super easy to invest in international markets. When a fund invests overseas, it faces an additional layer of risk – currency fluctuations. This plays a role in global ETFs because returns earned on overseas investments need to be converted back into Aussie dollars. That's when the impact of currency movements can be felt.

Let's look at a simple example of how currency risk works. We'll say Kylie buys units in an ETF that invests in the Japanese sharemarket. A year later, Japan's equity market has recorded gains of 20%. But over the same period, the yen has dropped in value by 15% relative to the Aussie dollar. In this case, the ETF's return is calculated as:

{20% index return} + {-15% currency loss} = 5% international return.

In other words, after taking currency movements into account, Kylie's fund records a 5% return.

This can work the other way as well. Kylie's ETF could have made a 30% gain on the Japanese sharemarket at a time when the yen rose 10% in relation to the Aussie dollar. In that case, Kylie's ETF would have notched up a 40% return.

The impact of currency movements can be managed through 'hedging'. This refers to strategies used by the fund manager to offset the impact of currency fluctuations. Hedging can mean the fund experiences less volatile returns. But the returns on an unhedged ETF have the potential to be higher if currency markets move in your favour.

Choosing between the two can come down to how you feel about risk. Bear in mind, too, that some pundits believe that over long periods of time, currency fluctuations even themselves out, which means how long you plan to hold onto your international ETF can also impact your choice. One possible solution is to take an each-way bet and have some hedged ETFs in your portfolio, as well as exposure to unhedged funds.

8 things you need to know about ETFs

1. ETFs CAN BE TAX-EFFICIENT

Because ETFs aim to mirror a market index, the underlying investments may only need to be tweaked when the composition of the index alters. This means ETFs can have a low rate of turnover of their underlying investments. It's something which can work in an investor's favour as it means fewer capital gains are passed on to investors through their distributions, so you can potentially pay less tax.

2. FRANKING CREDITS CAN BE PASSED ON TO UNITHOLDERS

If your ETF invests in Aussie companies that pay franked dividends (dividends paid out of profits on which the company has paid tax), the franking credits can be passed on to unitholders, helping to make the ongoing distributions very tax-friendly.

3. ETFs ARE ELIGIBLE FOR A CAPITAL GAINS TAX DISCOUNT

Just like shares, if you hold on to the units in your ETF for more than 12 months, any profit you make on the sale of your units may be eligible for a 50% capital gains tax discount.

4. MOST ETFs ARE HIGHLY LIQUID

The ease and speed with which you can convert an investment back to cash is referred to as its liquidity. Being listed on the ASX means your units can often be traded in a matter of seconds.

5. TRANSPARENCY

It's easy to see at a glance what your investment in an ETF is worth at any time. ETF unit prices are available 24/7 via the ASX website, which provides tremendous transparency for investors.

6. TAX TIME CAN BE COMPLEX

If there is one drawback of ETFs, it's the paperwork that funds are required to issue at tax time. The annual tax statements tend to be lengthy documents. It is possible to complete your tax return yourself, but follow the tax statement. If in doubt, hand the paperwork over to your tax professional.

7. YOU MAY BE ABLE TO REINVEST DISTRIBUTIONS

Some ETFs let you purchase more units in the fund with distributions rather than getting a cash payment. Be aware, though, you will normally still pay tax on the payment as if it had been received in the hand.

8. THERE'S NOWHERE TO HIDE WITH A PASSIVELY MANAGED FUND

When you invest in a passively managed fund, you are accepting market returns – they aren't designed to beat the market. So, if the market that your ETF focuses on takes a bath in the red, the value of your investment will fall, too.

If you feel strongly that it's worth a shot at beating the market, an actively managed fund may suit you better. Remember, though, you're likely to pay higher fees and those fees apply no matter whether your fund turns in a winning result or dishes up a loss.

FAST FACT

ETHICAL ETFs HAVE BEEN GROWING IN POPULARITY. SUSTAINABLE ETFs LISTED ON THE ASX HAVE INCREASED 79% PER YEAR OVER THE PAST FIVE YEARS, ACCORDING TO STOCKSPOT. AS AT THE END OF MARCH THERE WAS ALMOST $1.7 BILLION INVESTED IN ETHICAL ETFs.

ACTION PLAN

☐ *Choose the index/asset type that you would like to track – maybe it is the ASX 200, property or international shares.*

☐ *Find ETFs that invest in that particular index or asset area. You can find a full list on the ASX website or check with your online broker if you have one.*

☐ *Take a look at how the various ETFs have performed compared to the index over the long term.*

☐ *Make sure the fees are not too high.*

☐ *Take a look at who manages the ETF and check that they are reputable.*

☐ *Remember diversification is important so if you keep building an ETF portfolio make sure to mix up the assets you are invested in.*

I CAN...

Buy an investment property

There's something about bricks and mortar that Australians love. Seven in 10 of us own our home, and more than 2.2 million investors own a rental property. With some planning and careful number crunching, you too could become a landlord. You certainly don't need to be a homeowner to get started, but unlike many other investments, buying a rental place means taking on a substantial debt. So, let's look at the nuts and bolts of becoming a property investor to help you decide if it's right for you.

How much deposit do you need to invest?

Just like buying a home, investors need a deposit plus enough cash to cover the property's upfront purchase costs. The difference is that saving a 20% deposit isn't as critical for investors. Loan interest can usually be claimed on tax, so there's less incentive to minimise the amount you borrow. And while a deposit below 20% will mean paying lenders mortgage insurance (LMI), the premium, along with other borrowing costs like loan application fees, can be claimed on tax over a five-year period.

The upshot is that investors are often keen to devote as little upfront cash to their purchase as possible, whereas the opposite can apply to home buyers.

If you're a homeowner you may not need to stump up much cash at all. Some lenders accept home equity in lieu of a cash deposit. This will mean the rental property is 100% funded by debt – so your cashflow needs to be able to handle the loan repayments – but using home equity this way can help to preserve cash savings.

Of course, not all investors are homeowners. So, let's see how much a hypothetical investor, Liz, may need to get started with a rental property. The numbers will vary between locations, but I've assumed Liz invests in a Melbourne apartment, paying $576,000.

Liz may be able to buy with a 10% deposit of $57,600. This will mean paying LMI of $16,278 – and she'll need to pay it as a lump sum rather than add it to the loan because she's already at the lender's maximum borrowing limit of 90%. After allowing for stamp duty and other upfront costs, Liz will need at least $105,638 to buy the apartment.

If Liz can put together a 20% deposit, equal to $115,200, she can avoid the cost of LMI. This will call for a bigger chunk of cash, though – $146,900 in total after allowing for other costs, and that means finding an extra $41,322.

You may be happy to wait and save a 20% deposit. But if values are rising rapidly, it can be cost-effective to pay LMI and get into the market sooner. Remember, the LMI premium can be claimed on tax over a five-year period, so the cost of getting into the market with a small deposit today may be recouped as tax savings later on.

$9,000
THE AVERAGE AMOUNT OF DEPRECIATION INVESTORS CAN CLAIM IN THE FIRST YEAR, ACCORDING TO BMT TAX DEPRECIATION.

Choosing your investment loan

Investment loans work in much the same way as regular home loans but there are a few features to look for as an investor.

THE LENDER'S DEPOSIT LIMITS While some lenders accept a 10% deposit on investment property loans, others prefer to see a deposit of 20%, in some cases, even 30%. If a 10% deposit is your preferred limit, it's worth speaking to a mortgage broker for help finding the right loan.

THE RATE Investment loans tend to come with higher rates than regular home loans. As I write, the average variable rate for owner-occupied loans is 2.69%, compared to 3.05% for investors. Loan interest may be tax deductible but it's still a major cost that will impact your returns, so it's worth shopping around for a competitive deal.

FIXED TERMS Loan features such as redraw and offset often are not as attractive to investors as they are to homeowners. This comes back to being able to claim loan interest on tax, which reduces the need to pay off the debt sooner. What's often more important for landlords is the ability to lock into a fixed rate, which provides certainty over a key expense.

OPTION TO MAKE INTEREST-ONLY PAYMENTS The option to make interest-only payments can be highly prized by investors as it lowers the regular repayments. The downside is the possibility of paying a higher rate – at the time of writing, interest-only rates averaged 3.17%.

Among lenders that offer interest-only, a time limit usually applies, generally three to five years. After this period, you'll need to renegotiate the interest-only arrangement with the lender, or start making principal plus interest payments.

HOW MUCH YOU CAN BORROW Most lenders will include rental income in their calculations when working out how much you can borrow. But you need hard evidence.

Ask the selling agent to put the property's estimated weekly rent in writing so that it can form part of your loan application. What's less likely is that the lender will include any possible tax savings in your loan application, so don't rely on this to get your loan application over the line.

Choosing the property that's right for you

The beauty of buying as an investor is that you don't have to choose a place based on personal needs or preferences. While this can considerably open up your options, be sure to buy with your head, not your heart. Focusing on four main criteria can help you make an informed decision.

1. LOCATION

As an investor you're free to explore regional areas (which can be affordable) or even interstate properties. The common thread is to look for locations with:

✓ A healthy and diverse local economy – this will underpin capital growth and provide employment prospects for tenants.

✓ Population growth – more residents means greater demand, and a bigger pool of tenants. The Australian Bureau of Statistics and local council websites can provide details of population trends.

✓ Abundant local facilities – especially schools and healthcare facilities backed by good transport links, which will appeal to tenants and future buyers.

✓ Low vacancy rates – a handy source of information is SQM Research, where you can check vacancy rates by postcode.

2. THE TYPE OF PROPERTY: APARTMENT VERSUS HOUSE

Apartments have plenty of pluses for investors. They tend to be low maintenance, which appeals to landlords and tenants; they are typically more affordable; and the rental yields are generally higher – 4.1% nationally compared to 3.7% for houses.

When it comes to capital growth, however, houses can hold the trump card. Traditionally, houses have enjoyed stronger rates of growth, reflecting the scarcity of land. On the flipside, apartments have become a lot more popular, owing to the low-maintenance lifestyle they provide. The deal breaker, however, can be the sheer number of apartments in a location.

Since 2015, our cities have seen a steep rise in the number of newly built apartments. As Table 1 shows, that's seen unit values lag behind houses in all but two state capitals – Sydney and Hobart. This highlights the need to look at the number of existing or planned apartments in any area you're looking to buy in. A high volume of units doesn't only impact capital growth, it can push down weekly rents and make it harder to attract a tenant.

TABLE 1 CAPITAL GROWTH APARTMENTS VERSUS HOUSES 2015-2020

	MEDIAN VALUE 30 JUNE 2015[1]		MEDIAN VALUE 30 JUNE 2020[2]		5-YEAR GROWTH	
	Apartment	House	Apartment	House	Apartment	House
Sydney	$650,000	$900,000	$761,792	$1,010,426	17.20%	12.27%
Melbourne	$480,000	$615,000	$575,009	$802,551	19.79%	30.50%
Brisbane	$382,000	$487,500	$387,420	$557,265	1.42%	14.31%
Canberra	$420,000	$590,000	$444,181	$716,150	5.76%	21.38%
Hobart	$265,000	$347,500	$399,404	$516,600	50.72%	48.66%
Adelaide	$337,200	$430,000	$332,016	$476,639	-1.54%	10.85%
Perth	$425,000	$525,000	$357,379	$459,376	-15.91%	-12.50%
Darwin	$463,500	$585,000	$271,757	$470,136	-41.37%	-19.63%

[1] *CoreLogic June RP Data Hedonic Home Value Index Results, 1 July 2015.*
[2] *CoreLogic Hedonic Home Value Index, 1 July 2020.*

3. NEW VERSUS OLD

A new property may appeal to landlords because there are likely to be lower repair and maintenance bills, but the number one attraction by far is a much larger depreciation claim.

Depreciation refers to the steady decline in value over time of a building as well as 'fixtures and fittings' such as stoves, hot water heaters, light fittings and even flooring. Investors love depreciation because it's a non-cash expense. In other words, you get a tax deduction without having to dip into your pocket.

In 2017, the tax rules were changed so that the depreciation can no longer be claimed on previously used items (for instance, appliances) in established properties. In a brand new property, nothing has been used, which translates into a more generous tax deduction.

To be sure you're maximising this deduction, it's worth having a depreciation schedule drawn up by a quantity surveyor. This can cost up to $1,000 but it's also tax deductible.

The property you select should reflect your goals. If you're looking for extra income, rental yield may be the main game. If you're keen on capital growth – and you're prepared to hold onto the place for the long term (at least five to seven years) – then picking a property with growth prospects is the key.

It's an important distinction because, in general, locations that deliver high price growth often have modest rental yields, and vice versa.

In Sydney, for instance, property prices (across all types of dwellings) have climbed 66.7% over the past decade – the highest nationwide.

But as Table 2 shows, the rental yield is also the lowest across our state capitals. Conversely, cities that have seen lower rates of capital growth have higher rental yields.

TABLE 2 **LONG-TERM PROPERTY PRICE VALUES VERSUS RENTAL YIELD**

	SYDNEY	**MELBOURNE**	**BRISBANE**	**ADELAIDE**
Change in property values – 10 years to 31 December 2019	66.7%	53.5%	8.5%	16.8%
Rental yield	3.0%	3.3%	4.5%	4.4%

	PERTH	**HOBART**	**DARWIN**	**CANBERRA**
Change in property values – 10 years to 31 December 2019	-14.1%	39.1%	-25.7%	24.5%
Rental yield	4.3%	5.1%	5.9%	4.6%

Source: CoreLogic Hedonic Home Value Index, January 2020.

Negative and positive gearing

'Gearing' simply means borrowing to invest. 'Negative gearing' occurs when the annual rent from a property is less than the costs of holding the place. The property makes a loss each year, which can be offset against other income, including your wage, to lower your annual tax bill.

A rental property can also be positively geared, meaning the rent you receive outweighs the expenses. When this happens, you're likely to end up owing tax at the end of each year.

To see the different impact of negative and positive gearing, let's look at another hypothetical example of Lucy, who earns an annual salary of $80,000 on which she pays tax (plus Medicare) of $19,147.

Now we'll see what happens if Lucy buys a rental property. She receives rent of $25,000 and pays annual costs of $35,000. As Table 3 shows, this loss will reduce Lucy's taxable income to $70,000, cutting her overall tax bill to $15,697, and giving Lucy a tax saving of $3,450.

Let's take a look at the situation if Lucy's investment is positively geared. We'll assume she still receives $25,000 annual rent but the yearly costs are $20,000, so she makes an annual profit of $5,000. This increases her taxable income to $85,000, so she'll owe $1,725 to the ATO.

TABLE 3 **TAX IMPACT OF NEGATIVE AND POSITIVE GEARING**

	NO RENTAL PROPERTY	NEGATIVELY GEARED RENTAL PROPERTY	POSITIVELY GEARED RENTAL PROPERTY
Salary	$80,000	$80,000	$80,000
Rental income/ (loss)	Nil	-10,000	$5,000
Taxable income	$80,000	$70,000	$85,000
Tax plus Medicare	$19,147	$15,697	$20,872
Tax saving		$3,450	-$1,725

Trimming your tax bill should never be the driving force behind an investment but the idea of using a rental property to save on tax tends to be ingrained in views on property investing. However, the tax savings only come about because the property is dishing up a loss. That's not what successful investing is all about. This is why it is so important to look for a property with real potential to grow in value over time, otherwise the only real sweetener is annual tax savings.

Knowing the costs you can claim

If you're a homeowner, you'll be aware that properties come with a whole variety of ongoing expenses. It can seem as though you're always dipping into your pocket. It's exactly the same with a rental property. The difference is that many of these ongoing costs can be claimed on tax. The main tax-deductible expenses include:

- Accounting fees

- Advertising for a new tenant

- Body corporate fees/strata levies (for apartments)

- Council and water rates (tenants normally pay for water consumption)

- Depreciation

- Insurances

- Land tax

- Loan interest

- Maintenance

- Pest control

- Property management

- Repairs

You will need written evidence of the costs you claim, so be prepared to maintain good records. Talk to your accountant to know exactly what you can – and cannot – claim in any given year.

HOW TO ATTRACT AND KEEP GOOD TENANTS

One of the best ways to protect your investment is to make sure you choose the right tenants and hold onto the good ones.

RESEARCH RENTAL PRICES

Make sure you are realistic about what rent to charge and try keep rent hikes competitive as you don't want to lose good tenants.

PRESENT PROPERTY NICELY

A property that looks well-presented is more likely to attract good tenants and get you a good rent.

CONSIDER ALLOWING PETS

Having a pet-friendly property may give you an edge on the competition.

THINK ABOUT FEATURES THAT COULD ENTICE TENANTS

Storage, built-in wardrobes, dishwashers and outdoor storage are some of the things to consider offering.

USE AN EXPERIENCED PROPERTY MANAGER

A good property manager can help you find great long-term tenants. They have access to a database that can help identify tenants with a bad history.

RESPOND TO REQUESTS FOR REPAIRS QUICKLY

Not only will you keep the tenants happy but you are making sure you are taking care of the property and maintaining its value.

How to own an investment property for the price of a weekly takeaway coffee

As I write in 2020, interest rates are at historic lows. This has significantly reduced one of the biggest costs of a rental property, and with some research, you could find a place that lets you invest for the price of a weekly coffee.

To see how this can work, let's meet another hypothetical investor – Tania, who buys an older house in Brisbane for $550,000 – close to the median value. In Queensland, land tax doesn't apply on properties below $600,000, so this is one cost Tania won't have to worry about.

The rental yield on the house is 4.3% – the average for Brisbane, which would make the rent about $450 per week. It takes two weeks for Tania to secure a tenant, so we'll say her rental income for the year is $22,500.

Tania put down a 20% deposit ($110,000) on the property, so she didn't pay LMI. However, the loan application fees came to $800, which she can claim over five years, or $160 annually. Her loan of $440,000 comes with a rate of 3.17%, bringing Tania's interest cost to $13,948 for the year.

As the house is old it requires some repairs and ongoing maintenance to keep it in good shape – I've allowed $2,000 for the year, plus an extra $600 for garden care. I had a quick hunt around online to get an idea of the typical costs for rates (council: $1,400 and water: $400) and landlord insurance ($1,000).

Tania uses a property manager to look after the place. The manager charges the equivalent of the first two weeks' rent as a letting fee ($900), plus an ongoing management fee of 9%, which works out to $2,025 for the year. I'll also allow $250 for miscellaneous expenses such as phone calls, internet and stationery, plus $600 for the extra cost Tania pays her accountant to prepare her tax return as a landlord.

As the house is older, I have taken a very conservative approach to depreciation, making allowance for $1,200 to be claimed over the year.

Finally, I'm going to assume Tania's marginal tax rate (including Medicare) is 34.5%. This means her annual income could range from $37,002 to $90,000.

TABLE 4 HOW AN INVESTMENT PROPERTY CAN COST LESS THAN A WEEKLY TAKEAWAY COFFEE

RENTAL INCOME	$22,500 A YEAR
Accounting fees	$600
Bank fees	$200
Borrowing expenses	$160
Gardening	$600
Landlord insurance	$1,000
Letting fee	$900
Loan interest	$13,948
Maintenance and repairs	$2,000
Property management	$2,025
Council rates	$1,400
Water rates	$400
Miscellaneous	$250
TOTAL CASH EXPENSES	**$23,483**
Pre-tax cash outflow	$983
Less depreciation	$1,200
LOSS FOR THE YEAR	**$2,183**
Marginal tax rate	34.5%
REFUND DUE	**$753**
TANIA'S CASH FLOW Total cash received – rent plus tax refund	$23,253
TOTAL CASH PAID OUT	$23,483
NET CASH OUTFLOW (CASH RECEIVED LESS CASH PAID OUT)	$230
WEEKLY CASH OUTFLOW	$4.42

So, let's look at Table 4 on page 165 to see how things shape up. Over the year Tania receives rent of $22,500 and pays out a total of $23,483 in cash expenses. This leaves her out of pocket by $983. However, after claiming depreciation, Tania would be due a tax refund of $753. If we add this to rental income of $22,500, Tania has pocketed $23,253 from the property during the year. On the other side of the ledger, she has paid out $23,483. This difference between her cash receipts and her cash outgoings for the year is $230. That works out to about $4.50 weekly – the price of a cappuccino.

FAST FACT

IT PAYS TO USE THE 'RENTAL YIELD' RATHER THAN THE DOLLAR VALUE OF WEEKLY RENT TO COMPARE DIFFERENT PROPERTIES. THE YIELD SHOWS THE ANNUAL RENT AS A PERCENTAGE OF THE PROPERTY'S CURRENT MARKET VALUE. IF AN APARTMENT IS VALUED AT $500,000 AND IS RENTED FOR $480 PER WEEK, THE ANNUAL RENT WILL BE $24,960, SO THE PROPERTY HAS A YIELD OF 4.9% ($24,960 ÷ $500,000 X 100).

Is property the right choice for you?

Based on Tania's example above, it can be very compelling to dive into the property market. Bear in mind, though, interest rates may not always be at record lows and you need to be able to handle the costs of owning your rental property when rates are high, during the inevitable vacancy periods, and still have some emergency cash for those times when the stove turns up its toes or the tenant floods the bathroom. Yes, a well-priced, carefully selected rental property can be a great long-term investment – and one that may be more affordable than you realise. Make sure you crunch the numbers, though, to be sure it's the right decision for you.

ACTION PLAN

☐ *Work out how much deposit you need.*

☐ *Think about whether you can use equity in an existing property as a deposit or whether you need to save.*

☐ *Explore loan options available to find one that has the features you need as an investor.*

☐ *To choose a property, consider the following: location; house versus apartment; new versus old; and whether you are chasing capital growth or yield.*

☐ *Develop a strong understanding of the tax benefits that may come with owning an investment property.*

☐ *Seek independent advice to help out with the numbers.*

I CAN...

Build my perfect portfolio

Building a portfolio is a lot like putting together a wardrobe of clothing. It's surprising how much the two have in common. Some investments will be evergreens that you'll want to hold on to for ages (just like those designer heels). Others will be selected to meet different needs (much like workwear or activewear). Importantly, your portfolio, like your wardrobe, should reflect who you are in terms of your goals, needs and life stage.

The main point is that if you can put together a decent wardrobe, you can certainly build a portfolio of investments. Here's what to look at.

Three key factors to consider

When you first set out as an investor, it can be confusing deciding which investments to include in your portfolio. Three factors can help to narrow down the choice.

1. HOW YOU FEEL ABOUT RISK

One of the main issues that should shape the investments you select is how you feel about risk.

All investments come with some sort of risk, so it's not something you can, or even should, try to avoid altogether. It's about finding the level of risk you are comfortable with. That said, the lower the risk, the lower your returns will be. And, if you want to earn higher returns, be prepared to take on more risk.

This risk-return trade-off is one of the ground rules of investing. You could, for example, play it safe by only investing in cash-based assets like savings accounts. The drawback is that you'll earn some very ho-hum returns.

Further along the scale are fixed-interest investments like government and corporate bonds, which have slightly more risk, but also the potential to deliver better returns. Both property and shares have a higher level of risk again. The pay-off for taking on that extra risk is the prospect of earning better long-term returns.

At the far end of the spectrum are speculative, or 'alternative', investments. These tend to be complex and extremely risky. I'm talking about things like futures, foreign currency and even cryptocurrencies like Bitcoin. Get it right with these, and you could pocket impressive returns. The reality, however, is that not many people do get it right and plenty end up losing money. That's not my idea of investing. I recommend skipping the speculative end of the spectrum unless you really know what you're doing.

Understanding how you feel about risk can call for a bit of soul searching. We all want to earn decent returns, but you need to feel comfortable about how your money is invested. If in doubt, think about whether your portfolio will pass the 'sleep test'. If concerns about a 10% downturn in the sharemarket will keep you awake at night, it could be worth cranking down the risk a notch or two even if it means accepting lower returns.

2. WHAT YOU WANT FROM YOUR INVESTMENTS

Next, think about why you are investing. Are you hoping to earn extra income; do you have a goal you're working towards like paying for your kids' education; or are you simply aiming to grow long-term wealth? The 'why' in your investment decision should have a bearing on what your portfolio looks like.

If you're looking for additional income, for instance, a term deposit can tick the box. The trouble is that the value of your money won't grow over time. So, it could pay to add shares to your portfolio. Dividends can be a source of regular income, and you'll also have the potential for capital growth as your shares rise in value over time. The bottom line is to look for the combination of investments that meet your needs and help you achieve your goals.

Your life stage can be the final clincher that shapes your portfolio. As a general rule, we can afford to take on more risk when we're young, and steadily dial down risk as we age. It's a view based on the idea that as we get older, we have fewer years ahead to recoup any losses.

The catch with this approach is if you're aged in your 50s or 60s, you could still have another 30 or so years ahead of you. On that basis, it can make sense to have some growth assets in your portfolio, so that your investments continue to outpace inflation.

Mix 'n' match – why diversifying matters

There are no set rules about what your portfolio should look like. But one thing's for sure: it makes a lot of sense to spread your money across a variety of investments. This is called 'diversification', and it works in your favour by reducing your portfolio's overall level of risk while smoothing out returns.

It's an effective strategy because investment markets don't all behave in the same way at the same time. When sharemarkets are up, for example, the property market may be down. Or when returns on cash are high, shares may be in the doldrums. Sure, it'd be great to pick the investments that do well every year. But in the absence of a crystal ball, no-one can say for sure which investment is about to take off, or which is about to head south. And over short periods of time, investment markets can be especially unpredictable.

We saw in 2020 how hard it can be to predict market outcomes. By way of background, at the end of 2019, Australian shares had enjoyed a cracking run, delivering total returns (capital gains plus dividends) of 25% for the year. On that basis, it would have seemed logical to invest heavily in shares. But just a few weeks into 2020, the Covid-19 pandemic hit, plunging Australia into lockdown and driving the sharemarket down by 36% in the space of four weeks between February and March.

An investor with all their money in shares would have done well in 2019, but the events of 2020 meant they would have taken a serious hit to their portfolio just a few months later. By contrast, an investor with a more diverse portfolio would have pocketed some of the gains on shares in 2019, but been shielded from the worst of the losses.

The key takeaway is that spreading your portfolio is a proven way to reduce risk without sacrificing healthy long-term returns.

For the record, diversifying doesn't mean simply investing across a number of asset classes. It's also possible to spread your money around different markets. When it comes to shares, for instance, investors can diversify across companies, industries and even geographic regions.

What's the ideal blend?

I mentioned earlier that your portfolio will be as unique as you are. And it should certainly reflect your appetite for risk, your investment goals, and your life stage, which means that deciding the right mix of investments for your portfolio is a very personal issue. If you're completely stumped, a professional financial advisor can recommend a portfolio tailored to your needs, though this will come at a cost.

Another approach is to follow the lead of professional fund managers, including super funds, which often build three main types of portfolios: conservative, balanced and growth.

Fund manager Vanguard has done some interesting research in this area. It looked at the returns and risks associated with several types of portfolios based on investment market results, spanning 1926 to 2018 – a period of 93 years.

As Table 1 shows, Vanguard found that a conservative portfolio would have recorded average annual returns of 6.6%. It's not a huge return but the sweetener is that losses were recorded in only 13 of the 93 years.

At the other end of the spectrum, a higher-risk growth portfolio would have earned a much better return, averaging 9.4% annually. The downside is that the portfolio would have copped a loss one in every four years.

Happily, there is a middle ground. A balanced portfolio would have notched up returns averaging 8.2% annually, with losses likely in one

TABLE 1 HOW DIFFERENT PORTFOLIO MODELS HAVE PERFORMED IN THE PAST

	PORTFOLIO MAKE-UP	AVERAGE ANNUAL RETURN	NUMBER OF YEARS WITH A LOSS
Conservative	Fixed interest 80% Shares 20%	6.6%	13 of 93
Balanced	Fixed interest 50% Shares 50%	8.2%	18 of 93
Growth	Fixed interest 20% Shares 80%	9.4%	24 of 93

Source: Vanguard portfolio allocation models.

in every five years. For many investors a balanced portfolio can be the Goldilocks option – not too risky, not too low with returns, and just right overall.

Vanguard's findings are based on a simple portfolio containing just two types of investments. I'd certainly like to see you have more than fixed-interest securities or shares in your own portfolio. Nonetheless, it does provide some guidelines that you may want to apply to your portfolio to find a balance between risk and return.

The 5 must-knows

There are five extra pointers when putting together your perfect portfolio.

1. PERSONALISE YOUR PORTFOLIO – DON'T COPY SOMEONE ELSE'S

We have all met those 'experts' who insist on sharing stories about how they've made huge returns on their investments. You are not one of them. You wouldn't copy someone else's wardrobe, so don't try to replicate someone else's investment portfolio.

2. FOLLOW A PLAN, NOT YOUR EMOTIONS

When it comes to investing, there's no place for FOMO or 'gut instinct'. Know what you're aiming for, stay focused on your goals, and don't let knee-jerk reactions shape your portfolio.

3. INCLUDE GROWTH INVESTMENTS

Over a period of 30 years, inflation of just 3% can reduce the purchasing power of your money by more than 50%. That means growth investments can play a valuable role in your portfolio at just about every life stage.

4. DON'T RELY ON PAST RETURNS

No-one can predict how asset markets will move and last year's winning investment often becomes this year's also-ran. Pick investments that you believe are right for you rather than focusing on yesterday's chart-toppers.

5. NOTHING STAYS THE SAME

Life doesn't stand still for long and you could experience any number of twists in the road: a career change, the end of a relationship, a big promotion, maybe even redundancy. So, chances are that your portfolio will need a few course corrections over time.

In fact, it's a good idea to take a look at your portfolio at least annually to be sure it still ticks all the boxes for how you feel about risk, your goals and where you're at in your life.

That's different from continually tinkering with your portfolio. But a steady, planned approach will help you maintain the mix of investments that remains right for you over time.

FAST FACT

DON'T CHASE LAST YEAR'S WINNER. ACCORDING TO VANGUARD IN 2019, AUSTRALIAN LISTED PROPERTY, FOR EXAMPLE, WAS THE BEST PERFORMING ASSET CLASS, DELIVERING A RETURN OF 19.3%. IN THE YEAR TO 30 JUNE 2020, THE VERY SAME SEGMENT WAS THE WORST PERFORMER, PRODUCING A NEGATIVE RETURN OF 21.3%.

ACTION PLAN

☐ *Get to know yourself. Consider how you feel about risk, what you want from your investments and your stage in life.*

☐ *Educate yourself on the various investment options, how they work and the possible risks.*

☐ *Start by investing in something you feel comfortable with, which might be direct shares, an ETF or managed fund, fixed interest or property to name a few.*

☐ *Keep adding to your portfolio and remember to mix and match so that you have some level of diversification.*

☐ *Get professional advice if you need it.*

☐ *Revisit your portfolio on a regular basis to make sure it still meets your needs or if any adjustments are needed.*

I CAN...

Retire on $50,000 a year

I love my career and I love raising a family but, hey, I'm also looking forward to retirement. And I certainly have no intention of swapping vintage reds for something that comes in a cardboard box, or spending holidays at a hostel rather than in a fancy hotel. Quite simply, I want my retirement to be as fulfilling as my working life – and I want yours to be, too. But it won't happen by chance for either of us.

A decent retirement demands one thing: sufficient money to pay for it all. The only way we can be sure of living on a good income in retirement is to plan ahead for it.

There's no getting around the fact that saving for retirement means giving up some cash today. The earlier you start, the less you need to tuck away – that's all thanks to the power of the compounding returns I spoke about in Chapter 11: I can invest with just $100 a week. But even if you've left your run a bit late, there are ways to give your retirement nest egg a final boost.

Let's have a look at the steps you can take to whoop it up in retirement on an income of $50,000 annually.

Why $50,000?

One question I'm often asked is, 'How much money do I need in retirement?' I've come across research that suggests aiming for a retirement income equal to 70% of your final working salary.

The problem is that this isn't always relevant in today's environment where many Australians steadily wind down their working week ahead of full-time retirement.

A different approach is to use the quarterly ASFA Retirement Standard. It provides a benchmark for the annual budget needed to fund a 'comfortable' as well as a 'modest' standard of living in retirement.

As Table 1 shows, in mid-2020 a single retiree needs an annual income of $43,687 to lead a comfortable lifestyle or around $27,902 for a modest lifestyle. Both are based on owning a home. I'm going to bypass the modest option because, frankly, you deserve better. ASFA's definition of 'modest' means occasional cheap eats, budget haircuts, and rare trips to the cinema. That's not the sort of retirement I want for you.

ASFA's notion of a 'comfortable' retirement is a little better, with plenty of holidays, fine dining and regular leisure activities.

TABLE 1 **BUDGETS FOR VARIOUS LIVING STANDARDS IN RETIREMENT (AGED AROUND 65)**

	MODEST LIFESTYLE		COMFORTABLE LIFESTYLE	
	Single	Couple	Single	Couple
Total per year[1]	$27,902	$40,380	$43,687	$61,909

[1] As at June 2020

Source: ASFA Retirement Standard. This assumes you own your own home.

But why settle for comfortable? Let's aim higher because if you can live well in retirement on $43,687, you're going to have a great lifestyle with an annual income of $50,000.

I realise that $50,000 may not sound like much when you're in the workforce. But bear in mind, seniors can tap into some very handy tax breaks. If the bulk of your income comes from superannuation savings, it can be tax-free from age 60. Your living costs should also be much lower. Your (by then) adult kids will, hopefully, be independent, you won't have to fork out for work-related costs like transport, and one of the biggest expenses of your working life – your home loan – should be behind you. Long story short, for a retiree, $50,000 can go a long way.

Why super is such a great retirement investment

Australia's retirement income system is based on several 'pillars': home ownership, superannuation, investments held outside of super, and the age pension. At the time of writing we were still waiting for the Retirement Income Review.

It's a no-brainer that owning your home is a plus in retirement. If you can clear the home loan by the time you exit the workforce, every dollar of income can go straight to your lifestyle and not your lender.

And, of course, I want you to build a portfolio of investments throughout your working life – be it ETFs, shares, or whatever combination of assets works for you. However, from the moment most of us enter the workforce, a valuable ultra-long-term investment starts to build behind the scenes. I'm talking about superannuation.

For many Australians, super is something that goes largely overlooked during their working lives. That goes a long way to explaining why there is almost $21 billion in lost and unclaimed super across Australia. But there's a lot to love about super. Your employer will chip in 9.5% of your base wage or salary each year in 'concessional' or before-tax contributions, which are taxed at just 15%. The returns on super are also lightly taxed.

You can (and should) add to super from your own pocket. This can be done using before-tax income via salary sacrifice – more on this later. Or you can make contributions out of your own pocket, which can usually be claimed on tax, up to a maximum of $25,000 annually.

This $25,000 annual limit includes your boss's 9.5% contributions plus your own salary sacrifice contributions. So if your employer adds, say, $15,000 to your fund annually, you have the option to chip in another $10,000 and claim it as a tax deduction.

If your before-tax super contributions reach the $25,000 annual limit, it's possible to make additional after-tax contributions from your own pocket – up to $100,000 annually. The beauty of these non-concessional contributions is that they aren't taxed at all within your fund.

The best part of super happens after age 60. Once you reach 'preservation age' you can withdraw your super as a lump sum payment, or keep it in the super system and use the money to invest in a 'retirement income stream'.

It's a way of having your super savings drip-fed to you through regular payments like a wage or salary. The real plus is that by keeping your money in the super system this way, you'll pay no tax on investment earnings, income payments or any lump sum withdrawals you choose to take.

The catch with super is that unless you are a high income earner, your employer's contributions alone may not be enough to build a nest egg that will generate annual income of $50,000. That's why it pays to look at ways you can grow your super savings for tomorrow without too much impact on today's cash flow.

I mentioned a fourth pillar of retirement funding – the age pension. It too can play a role in earning that $50,000 post-work income.

60
THE AGE YOU CAN ACCESS YOUR SUPER IF YOU WERE BORN AFTER 30 JUNE 1964.

As at August 2020, the age pension for a single person is worth a maximum of $944.30 per fortnight or $24,552 annually. It's possible to receive a full age pension if you own up to $268,000 in other assets including your super, though excluding your home.

But you can still be eligible for a part pension even if you have up to $583,000 in assets. This is important because when you begin to draw income out of your super, the balance of your fund can steadily decline.

As this happens, your eligibility for a part-pension can increase and, as we'll see, the age pension can supplement your super-based income.

Growing your super to achieve a $50,000 income

To demonstrate some of the potential strategies you can use to live on $50,000 a year in retirement, we'll take a look at three hypothetical women of different ages – Gina (30), Samantha (45) and Nicole (55). I've assumed their age at retirement is 67, and a potential life expectancy of 85, which is the average for Australian women. I've also assumed these women are single. That's deliberate. A man is not a financial plan and even if you're happily partnered, it's still handy to know what you can do to independently grow your retirement savings.

It's also worth pointing out that I've crunched the numbers based on the super and age pension rules as they apply in 2020. If you're aged in your 20s or 30s, it's a fair bet these will change, possibly substantially, by the time you reach your 60s. However, it's estimated that by 2055 one in four Australians will be aged 65 years or older, so while the rules of super may alter, the Federal Government is likely to make it more, not less, attractive for Australians to set aside money for retirement.

Gina, aged 30

Let's meet Gina. She's aged 30 and earns the average income for this age group – $58,635 annually. Gina has accumulated modest super savings of $21,765 – again the average for women in her age group. Like all the women here, we'll say her salary rises by 1.5% annually.

If Gina sticks with her employer's compulsory super contributions worth 9.5% of her salary, she's likely to have super savings of $410,813 by age 67. This would give her a retirement income of $40,484 annually. Not bad, but still about $10,000 short of our $50,000 target.

A simple way for Gina to ramp up her nest egg is by salary sacrificing additional super contributions. This involves having part of her before-tax salary paid into her super fund instead of receiving the money as cash in hand.

To grow her super to a level where she can expect a retirement income of $50,000 annually, Gina will need to salary sacrifice 6% of her before-

GRAPH 1 **GINA'S RETIREMENT INCOME MIX – AGE 67-84**

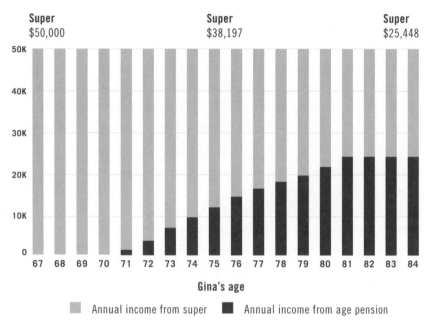

Source: *MoneySmart Retirement Income Planner*

tax pay to super each year from age 30. By following this routine, Gina's super savings will reach $595,000 by age 67 – sufficient to fund a yearly income of $50,000 through to age 85.

Gina's retirement income won't always be comprised solely of drawdowns from her super. Graph 1 shows that as Gina's super balance whittles away from age 67, she will become increasingly eligible for a slice of the age pension. By age 75, her income will be a blend of $38,197 from super with the balance of $11,803 coming from the age pension. By age 84, it will be almost a 50:50 mix.

The question is, how will giving up 6% of her before-tax salary affect Gina's take-home pay? After all, she needs sufficient cash for today's needs. The answer is that the impact can be surprisingly low.

On Gina's annual salary of $58,635, she'll pay tax plus Medicare totalling $11,776. This leaves her with after-tax pay of $46,859 or about $900 in the hand each week. By salary sacrificing 6% of her before-tax pay, in the first year she'll add an extra $3,518 to her super. This will take her taxable salary down to $55,117, on which she'll pay tax plus Medicare of $10,562, leaving her with after-tax income of $44,555, or $856 cash in hand each week. That's a difference of just $44. By contrast, if Gina were to add $3,518 to her super using after-tax income, she would have to give up $68 of her net pay each week. In this way it's easy to see how salary sacrifice is such a compelling way to grow super.

Samantha, aged 45

So, you're not in your 30s. Okay, let's crunch the numbers for Samantha, aged 45. Again, she earns the average annual income for that age group of $78,192, and has the average super balance for women in their 40s, which is $67,243.

Relying only on her employer's compulsory (9.5%) contributions will see Samantha accumulate a retirement fund of $349,536 by age 67. This will give her an annual income of $42,946 (with $10,515 of this coming from the age pension), which once again is short of our $50,000 target. So, Samantha decides to make additional contributions of her own.

Samantha may start out with more in super than Gina but she has less time remaining to grow her balance. This being the case, she will need to salary sacrifice super contributions of around 9% of her before-tax salary in each remaining year to accumulate super of $531,680, which will generate a retirement income of $50,000 annually. Here, too, over time the age pension will kick in to add to Samantha's super drawdowns.

Nicole, aged 55

By now you're probably seeing a pattern. The closer you are to retirement, the more you'll need to add to super yourself to ramp up your nest egg to achieve a healthy post-work income. That's the case for our hypothetical 55-year-old Nicole, who earns the average annual income of $80,298, and has $118,408 in super – also the average for a woman her age. With just 12 years before retirement at age 67, Nicole faces some stiff challenges to lift her super savings. But it can be done.

If she relies only on her employer's super contributions, she can expect to accumulate $277,324 by age 67, which will fund an annual income of just over $41,000. To have sufficient super to pocket a retirement income of $50,000 annually, Nicole needs to add to her nest egg through salary sacrifice, personal contributions or a combination of both.

She could, for instance, make salary sacrifice contributions worth 13% of her pre-tax salary, then chip in an additional $120 per week of her after-tax wage. This would see her retire with $504,926 in super, enough to generate yearly income of $50,000.

That extra contribution of $120 weekly would work out to $6,240 annually and it could come from a combination of her annual tax refund, perhaps a work bonus, or just through a regular pattern of adding to her super.

Another option for Nicole is to take advantage of the 'downsizer' super contribution. From age 65, she can sell her home and contribute up to $300,000 from the sale proceeds to super as long as she has owned her home for at least 10 years.

Working out your own super savings sweet spot

Just as Gina, Samantha and Nicole can each use a mix of options to grow their super balances, you can too. It's about deciding the strategy that you can maintain consistently over the long term.

A financial planner can help you develop a super strategy. There are also plenty of free resources available to help you work out how to grow your nest egg including online calculators that will show the impact of regular contributions on your final super balance. The figures for the case studies in this chapter were based on the Retirement Planner calculator on the MoneySmart website.

ARE YOU ON TRACK FOR A COMFORTABLE RETIREMENT?

Take a look at how much you should have in super to reach the ASFA comfortable retirement standard of $545,000 and the gap based on average super balances.

$17,000 ($20,523)
$93,000 ($58,700)
$195,000 ($104,600)
$330,000 ($192,300)
$503,000 ($349,900)

GAP +$3,523
GAP -$34,300
GAP -$90,400
GAP -$137,700
GAP -$153,100

WHAT WOMEN SHOULD HAVE (WHAT WOMEN HAVE)

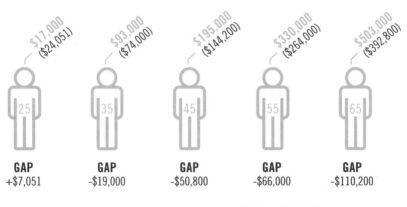

$17,000 ($24,051)
$93,000 ($74,000)
$195,000 ($144,200)
$330,000 ($264,000)
$503,000 ($392,800)

GAP +$7,051
GAP -$19,000
GAP -$50,800
GAP -$66,000
GAP -$110,200

WHAT MEN SHOULD HAVE (WHAT MEN HAVE)

Source: ASFA Super Detective calculator,
ASFA average superannuation account balances as at July 2019.

Your super fund's website is likely to have something similar. They're a useful tool to play around with the numbers to find the sweet spot of extra contributions that matches today's budget with your plans for the future. Many super funds also provide free general advice that can help you work out how to grow your super.

6 ways to add to your super

SALARY SACRIFICE Ask the boss to redirect part of your before-tax pay into super.

GOVERNMENT CO-CONTRIBUTIONS Make a personal super contribution of up to $1,000, and if you earn less than $53,564 you may be eligible for a government co-contribution. To get the maximum co-contribution of $500 you must earn less than $39,837 and add a total of $1,000 to your super fund

SPOUSE SUPER REBATE Your spouse/partner may be able to claim an 18% tax offset by making a contribution of up to $3,000 to your super fund if you're not working or you earn below $37,000 annually.

CONTRIBUTIONS MADE FROM AFTER-TAX MONEY Add up to $100,000 annually to your fund in after-tax (non-concessional) contributions. They can't be claimed on tax – but they aren't taxed once they hit your super fund.

DOWNSIZER CONTRIBUTIONS From age 65, sell a home you've owned for at least 10 years and add up to $300,000 of the sale proceeds to super ($300,000 each if you own the home with your spouse/partner).

PERSONAL CONTRIBUTIONS Up to $25,000 of before-tax super contributions can usually be claimed on tax. This annual limit includes your own salary sacrifice contributions plus the boss's 9.5% contributions.

5-point health check for your super

Adding to your super can make a big difference to your retirement lifestyle. But it's also possible to boost your super just by giving it a quick health check. Here's what to look at:

1. CHECK IF YOU HAVE LOST OR UNCLAIMED SUPER

Our super system is awash with unclaimed accounts, and yet it's easy to check if any of the $21 billion of lost super belongs to you. Jump onto the myGov portal (you'll need to link your account to the Taxation Office), or phone the ATO on 13 28 65. You'll need to have your tax file number handy. If it turns out you do have forgotten super savings, it costs nothing to transfer.

2. CHOOSE YOUR OWN FUND

Most workers are free to choose their own super fund and it's a good idea to do just that. The fund your employer selects may suit the boss but that doesn't mean it's right for you. Take a look online to compare different funds and when you've found a fund you like, pass the details onto your employer so that regular contributions can be paid into your account.

3. CONSIDER FOLDING MULTIPLE SUPER BALANCES INTO ONE ACCOUNT

Over 10 million Australians have more than one super fund. It means wasting money on fees. Rolling multiple balances into a single fund will stop this duplication and make it easier to keep track of your super during your working life. Sometimes it's worth having multiple funds if there are distinct benefits, such as cheap life insurance.

4. KNOW THE FUND FEES YOU'RE PAYING

Super funds charge a variety of fees – some are set as a percentage of your balance, others are based on a fixed dollar amount. On average, fees work out to between 0.94% and 1.28% of your account balance annually but you could pay as much as 2.73%. Check the fees you're paying and if your fund is at the high end of the scale, it could be worth switching to a less expensive fund.

5. UNDERSTAND HOW YOUR MONEY IS INVESTED

Your fund's underlying investment strategy will shape the returns your money earns and have a massive influence on your final balance.

The majority of Australians have their super in a balanced investment option, which spreads your money across a variety of assets, though often with up to 70% invested in shares. It is possible to choose other choices such as 'high growth', which will ramp up your exposure to sharemarkets and their potential for higher long-term returns.

Conversely, a 'conservative' strategy will see more of your money invested in low-risk/low-return investments such as cash and fixed interest.

The choice around how your super is invested will depend on how you feel about risk, and your life stage. Bear in mind that the same fund is unlikely to earn the highest returns every year. Ideally, look for a fund with a steady track record for strong returns coupled with low fees.

The time to start is now

Think about what matters to you and how you can achieve your retirement goals. We won't all retire as millionaires but, thankfully, financial security doesn't mean getting your name on the rich list.

I encourage you to take a fresh look at your super: how it's invested, the fees, and the strategies you can use to grow your retirement fund. Love your super today and your future is likely to be a lot more luxurious than it will be for those who spend their working years saying, "I'll get around to that one day".

FAST FACT

IF YOU WERE BORN IN 1980, YOUR SUPER BALANCE SHOULD BE CLOSE TO $154,000 IF YOU ARE HOPING TO BE ON TRACK FOR A 'COMFORTABLE' RETIREMENT, AS DEFINED BY ASFA. YOU CAN USE THE CALCULATOR AT SUPERGURU.COM.AU/ CALCULATORS/SUPER-DETECTIVE TO WORK OUT WHETHER YOU'RE ON TRACK OR HAVE SOME CATCHING UP TO DO.

ACTION PLAN

☐ *Decide how much you would like to live on at retirement – it may be more or less than the $50,000 a year I have assumed here.*

☐ *Use a calculator such as the Retirement Planner to estimate what income you're likely to get from super and the age pension when you retire.*

☐ *If you aren't on track to reach your target, play around with the numbers to work out how much you may need to contribute to hit your goal.*

☐ *Be careful not to go over the caps.*

☐ *Give your fund a health check – how has it performed and what are the fees? Making sure you are not paying too much and that your fund is delivering consistent returns can be one way to boost your balance without putting in an extra cent.*

☐ *Don't forget to factor in any other investments you own that may be able to give you regular income at retirement, such as an investment property.*

☐ *Be sure to seek expert independent financial advice.*

I CAN...

Find good advice

When a light bulb blows you probably change it yourself but if you need your entire house rewired then (I'd certainly hope) you'd call an electrician. And if you have a headache you might take some paracetamol but if it persists for a while then you would probably pay your GP a visit. The same should apply when it comes to money matters – there will be some things you can handle yourself but then there are others you could use a helping hand with – even if it means having to pay for it.

So who do you call when you need some advice and how do you find the right person? Let's take a look.

If you want advice on investments and building wealth ...

A FINANCIAL ADVISOR The main role of a financial advisor, often referred to as a financial planner, is to help you set financial goals and help you achieve them. Part of that may be helping you choose investments and building a diversified portfolio but they can also help with a range of other things such as life insurance, retirement planning, superannuation and estate planning.

You may also be able to get one-off advice on a particular issue rather than comprehensive advice based on your entire situation. For example, you may simply want advice on what to do with a redundancy payment or inheritance.

WHAT YOU NEED TO KNOW The Royal Commission into Misconduct in the Banking, Superannuation and Financial Services Industry revealed some harsh truths about the financial planning industry. Too many Aussies had received poor advice, were overcharged or were put into products that weren't right for them. It no doubt turned a lot of people off seeking advice.

But it's important not to tar all advisors with the same brush – there are still good ones out there. Start by asking for recommendations from family or friends. Another option is to find one who's a member of a professional organisation such as the Profession of Independent Financial Advisers (PIFA) or Financial Planning Association (FPA). Both their websites offer a tool which helps you find members near you.

Members of PIFA are considered independent because to join they have to satisfy the following criteria: no ownership links or affiliations with product manufacturers; no commissions or incentive payments from product manufacturers; and no-asset-based fees.

Make sure the advisor is licensed – you can check this using the 'Financial advisers register' on the MoneySmart website. It's also worth looking at the Financial Services Guide to find out who owns the company to ensure there are no conflicts of interest.

It can be a good idea to meet with a few different advisors to find one that you feel suits you. Most advisors won't charge for the initial meeting. Ask about their qualifications, how much experience they have, whether they have a specialty area and the types of product they offer (or don't offer) advice on. And of course ask about the fees.

As well as considering the answers to your questions, think about whether you felt comfortable with them.

THE COST Different advisors use different fee models. These can include commissions, asset-based fees, fee-for-service or performance-based fees. This is a question you should ask when looking for advisors.

To give you an idea CoreData FPA Member Research 2019 shows that on average it costs $2,671 for a financial plan if you're a new client. It's also worth noting that if you want continued support you'll probably be charged ongoing fees, which cost on average $3,757 a year.

A ROBO-ADVISOR A robo-advisor is basically automated online advice – you don't actually meet with a person. Generally you'll complete an online questionnaire which asks about your assets, how you feel about risk and your investment timeframe.

It will then recommend an investment portfolio, usually made up of different ETFs, based on your responses.

WHAT YOU NEED TO KNOW There are a number of platforms in Australia offering robo advice – the biggest are InvestSMART, Stockspot, Six Park and Quiet Growth.

When comparing your options think about how much you have to invest. Stockspot, for example, requires a minimum investment of $2,000, with additional investments of at least $1,000. Six Park requires a starting investment of $5,000.

Keep in mind that robo-advisors won't know everything about your personal financial situation so if you want a more holistic approach this might not be the best option for you.

THE COST How much you pay generally depends on the value of your portfolio. Stockspot, for example, charges $5.50 per month if your account balance is $10,000 or less, 0.055% per month or 0.66% per year if your account balance is between $10,001 and $200,000.

A good way to compare fees between providers is to work out how much you'd pay based on your current balance. Also find out if any additional fees apply.

If you want advice on super ...

YOUR SUPER FUND A financial advisor (see page 191) can generally help with advice on your superannuation but you may also be able to get help from your super fund.

WHAT YOU NEED TO KNOW There are generally three levels of advice offered by super funds. The first is non-ongoing personal advice on simple topics, also referred to as 'intra-fund' advice. Some of the topics that fall into this category include your investment and insurance options, your contribution options and consolidating super.

The next level is 'scaled' advice, which is limited to a particular topic such as working out the most effective contributions strategy for you. The third is comprehensive advice which may include financial matters outside of super.

Not all super funds offer all three levels of advice. It's best to contact your super fund to task what type of advice is available to you.

If you are getting comprehensive advice take the same care you would when choosing a financial advisor and ask about their qualifications, how they are paid and any specialty areas.

THE COST Intra-fund advice won't cost you anything because it is covered by the fees you and other members have already paid. The fees for scaled and comprehensive advice will vary between super funds but to give you an idea UniSuper says the fee for scaled advice is up to $205 per hour and typically the total fee is in the range of $530-$990.

For comprehensive advice UniSuper says it will cost about $300 per hour and generally the total fee will be in the range of $2,500-$6,000. It's worth noting that you may be able to pay any fees for advice from your super account. Again check with your super fund.

If you want advice on home loans ...

A MORTGAGE BROKER A good mortgage broker can help you find a loan that suits you and also does most of the hard work for you. Another plus is that they know the ins and outs of the industry and may be able to suggest a lender more likely to say yes.

WHAT YOU NEED TO KNOW Getting recommendations from family and friends can be a good way to narrow down your choices. Another option is to head to mortgageandfinancehelp.com.au, which will help you find a broker who is accredited with the major industry body, Mortgage & Finance Association of Australia (MFAA).

It can be a good idea to meet with a few on your shortlist. It's probably also a good idea to check if they are licensed before making any appointments.

There are a number of questions to ask, including how much experience they have, how many lenders are on their panel and who they are. Also ask how they are paid. For example do they get the same fee regardless of the loan or lender?

35%

OF AUSSIES SAY THE
REASON THEY DON'T
GET FINANCIAL
ADVICE IS BECAUSE
IT'S TOO EXPENSIVE,
ACCORDING TO A
REPORT BY ASIC,
AUGUST 2019.

It's important to note that some of the cheapest loans are not sold through brokers as they may not pay a commission, so it's important to do your own research too.

THE COST A mortgage broker generally won't cost you anything. Most make money by earning a commission from the financial institutions whose products they sell to clients.

If you want advice on property ...

A BUYER'S AGENT A buyer's agent can help home buyers or property investors find a property and can also assist with negotiating the sale or bidding at auction.

WHAT YOU NEED TO KNOW Some buyer's agents operate solely in the client's interests while others can receive commissions from selling property as well. It's important to make sure you are using a 'true' buyer's agent.

You can use the Real Estate Buyers Agents Association of Australia (REBAA) to find a buyer's agent near you. Make sure you check that they are licensed and find out how much experience they have in the area you are interested in.

THE COSTS Fees usually range from 1.5% to 3% of the property price. They may also charge a lower fee for limited services such as offering an appraisal or bidding at auction.

A PROPERTY ADVISOR A property advisor can provide a property investment plan tailored to your needs.

WHAT YOU NEED TO KNOW Ideally you should look for a Qualified Property Investment Advisor (QPIA), which means they have been trained by the peak industry body Property Investment Professionals of Australia (PIPA).

Find out how much experience they have and how much they'll charge. It can be a good idea to ask for a sample of the type of report you can expect.

THE COST Fees can range from $2,000 up to $10,000 for extensive multi-purchase property portfolio plans. Some work on a commission model though.

If you have money woes ...

A FINANCIAL COUNSELLOR A financial counsellor can help you if you are having trouble paying bills or are in debt.

WHAT YOU NEED TO KNOW All the information you give is confidential. They can help you develop a money plan, understand which debts are priorities, talk to creditors and let you know if you may be eligible for any grants and concessions.

A good starting point is the National Debt Helpline on 1800 007 007 or visit ndh.org.au.

THE COST Free.

FAST FACT

FEES FOR PREPARING A FINANCIAL PLAN (STATEMENT OF ADVICE) OR THE INITIAL INVESTMENT OR ADVICE FEES PAID TO ESTABLISH AN INVESTMENT ARE NOT TAX DEDUCTIBLE. FEES THAT RELATE TO ADVICE WHICH LEADS TO, OR IS DIRECTLY ASSOCIATED WITH, A SPECIFIC INVESTMENT THAT PRODUCES ASSESSABLE INCOME CAN BE CLAIMED.

ACTION PLAN

☐ *Think about the money issue you would like advice on and work out the best source of advice.*

☐ *Ask family, friends or colleagues if there is anyone they have used and trust.*

☐ *Check relevant professional organisations (if applicable) to find an expert near you.*

☐ *Consider meeting with a few experts to find one that feels right for you.*

☐ *Find out about any fees they charge.*

☐ *Have a goal in mind about what you would like to achieve with their help and be clear with them about it.*

☐ *After you receive advice it's a good idea to back it up with your own research.*

After 20 years of talking money, believe me when I say I've heard just about every money question. With that in mind I'd thought I'd share with you the top five questions that keep popping up time after time.

The recurring themes are property, shares, super and clearing debt. At the end of the day we all want the same thing ... to make the most of what we have. The good news is that the key to financial success is simple: do small things regularly. And to remember that when it comes to personal finance you need to keep it personal. The beauty about money is that there is no one right answer. Enjoy finding yours ... and, if needed, get some advice.

PART V

WHAT YOU'VE ALWAYS WANTED TO KNOW

—

SHOULD I PAY OFF MY HECS-HELP DEBT EARLY?

Chapter eighteen

Age certainly has its advantages. One of the perks of being as old as me is that when I got my degree in economics from the University of Queensland it was practically free. I didn't have to worry about repaying a HECS-HELP debt when I started working.

Younger generations aren't as fortunate. When they complete their university education, they might come out with a degree but they'll more than likely have a substantial HELP debt to repay.

A university education doesn't come cheap and many Aussie students can't or don't pay for it upfront. If you're eligible, the government will pay your course fees for you through the Higher Education Loan Program (HELP), which used to be known as the Higher Education Contribution Scheme (HECS). This is effectively a loan from the government.

Australian Taxation Office (ATO) figures show that the average amount of outstanding debt for the 2018-2019 financial year was $22,425.

What is a little scarier is that 244,201 people have debts higher than $50,000, with 22,514 of them owing more than $100,001.

When do I have to start repaying HECS-HELP?

The somewhat good news is you don't have to start repaying your HECS-HELP until your repayment income (RI) reaches a certain level.

The ATO explains that RI is taxable income plus any total net investment loss (which includes net rental losses), total reportable fringe benefits amounts, reportable super contributions and exempt foreign employment income. For the 2020-2021 financial year, this kicks in when your RI hits $46,620.

The amount you have to repay is set as a percentage of repayment income and can range from 1% to 10%. It will vary depending on what your RI is. For example, if you earn $46,620 to $53,826 your repayment rate is 1%, if you earn $67,955 to $72,031 it is 4% and if you earn $136,740 and above it is 10%. Visit ato.gov.au for more details.

According to the ATO, it takes people on average 9.2 years to repay their HELP debt, which makes you wonder whether it's a good idea to make voluntary repayments to clear it sooner. If you hate the idea of having the debt hanging over your head, this might feel like it is a good plan for you.

Funnily enough, there doesn't seem to be a huge financial incentive to pay it off quickly. Years ago, you would receive a discount for lump sum repayments but that's no longer the case.

Technically, you're not paying interest on the debt, but it is indexed in line with inflation on 1 June each year. This is applied to part of the loan that has remained unpaid for more than 11 months. The indexation rate for 2019 and 2020 was 1.8% but at the time of writing the rate for 2021 was not yet known.

It might not seem like a lot but it can add up over the long term. Let's say you finish uni with a $22,500 debt but your RI doesn't reach the threshold for three years. Assuming the debt is indexed at 1.8% a year, your debt would have increased by $1,237 to $23,737.

Two more reasons to consider paying off your HECS-HELP debt early are the facts that wage growth is practically non-existent and interest rates on savings accounts are so low at the moment.

Should I pay my HECS-HELP early?

The reality is that there is no single right answer. What is best for you might not apply to your siblings or friends. The decision will probably come down to a number of things. These include:

DO YOU HAVE ANY OTHER DEBTS? If you have any debts such as a personal loan, credit card or even a home loan where the interest rate you are being charged is higher than indexation then it's probably a good idea to direct any extra money towards clearing that first.

IS THERE SOMETHING ELSE YOU ARE SAVING FOR? You might have other financial goals that you want to achieve first. Maybe you want to save for a house deposit, invest in the sharemarket or even buy a car. If you feel that other goals are more important to you then you might choose to make those a priority.

CAN YOU GET A BETTER RETURN ON YOUR MONEY? Most savings accounts aren't paying much more than inflation. So, if you want to leave your money in a savings account but have no plans for the cash, it might be better to pay off your HECS-HELP debt. If you are willing to take on more risk though and invest in shares or ETFs, for example, you are likely to get a better return on your money.

Tip: If you plan on making a lump sum repayment towards your HECS-HELP debt, the best time to do this is before 1 June, when indexation is applied. That's because if the debt is smaller when the indexing is added the increase will effectively be lower. It's not going to be a huge saving but every little bit counts. It's probably best to do this at least one week in advance to allow enough time for the payment to be received and processed by the ATO before 1 June.

Will a HELP debt affect your home loan application?

You might also be wondering what it might mean to have a HECS-HELP debt if you plan on applying for a home loan. It will be treated as a debt when the lender is assessing your application and the fact that the compulsory repayments reduce your income will also be taken into account. This doesn't mean you won't be able to get a home loan but it may reduce the amount you can borrow.

SHOULD I BUY NOW AND PAY LMI OR WAIT UNTIL I HAVE A 20% DEPOSIT?

David and Michael want to buy a house but they don't have the full 20% deposit saved. Their question is: do they jump in now with their 10% deposit and pay the lenders mortgage insurance (LMI) or do they wait and save up more, taking the risk that by the time they've saved the full 20% deposit they're priced out of the market again?

It's a real dilemma. The answer, of course, depends on your personal situation and whether or not you believe prices are on the rise in the area you want to buy into. If prices are falling, it can turn out to be a very different story.

Lenders usually like you to have a deposit of at least 20% of the purchase price. So, if the property is worth $800,000, a 20% deposit would mean you'd have $160,000 saved.

Of course, you can save less and borrow more, but a lending valuation ratio of 80% or under (that's the amount of debt you have versus the value of the property) means you'd be up for LMI and this ain't cheap!

Typically, you can expect to pay around 2% of the loan amount for LMI. It's a one-off payment that protects the lender, not you, if you default on your loan.

Even then, if what you owe is greater than the sale price of your home, your lender is entitled to make a claim on the mortgage insurer for the reimbursement of any shortfall. The insurer can then go after you for this shortfall.

The cost of LMI can be paid as a lump sum, or some lenders may let you add it to your loan amount and pay it off with your loan repayments.

Keep in mind that if it's added to your loan you will pay interest on the cost of LMI.

It's worth noting that if you're a first home buyer and you qualify for the First Home Loan Deposit Scheme (FHLDS), you just may be able to avoid LMI altogether. The FHLDS allows first home buyers with deposits as low as 5% to get a home loan without paying LMI.

Essentially, the government will act as the mortgage insurer, guaranteeing home loans for eligible first home buyers with a minimum deposit of 5% of the property value. To be eligible, you will need to be earning less than $125,000 a year ($200,000 for a couple), and there are purchasing price thresholds which vary based on where you buy your property.

Back to Michael and David who, unfortunately, don't qualify for the FHLDS. The house they have their eye on is selling for $800,000. They have enough money saved to put down a 10% deposit and a bit extra to cover the additional costs such as stamp duty. Do they jump in now and pay LMI or wait and save?

The case for buying now and paying LMI

If David and Michael opt to buy that $800,000 home now with an $80,000 deposit they would be up for $17,712 LMI. They estimate it would take them a further five years to save an extra $80,000 to get the full 20% deposit, so they decide to jump in now and pay LMI.

They don't have enough money to pay for LMI upfront so they decide to add it to their loan – meaning their loan would be $737,712. Of course adding it to their mortgage means they'll have to pay interest on it.

TABLE 1 **BUYING NOW AND PAYING LMI**

	2020 (10% DEPOSIT)	2025 (20% DEPOSIT)
Purchase price	$800,000	$920,000
Deposit required	$80,000	$184,000
LMI	$17,712	-
Loan amount	$737,712	$736,000

Assuming the value of their house increases by 15% over the five years, the decision to buy now and pay LMI could work out well for them.

For starters, by the time they had saved $160,000 deposit they'd find themselves short again – this time by $24,000. That's because in 2025 that property would be worth $920,000 so they'd need $184,000 to make up a 20% deposit. And even though they had saved an extra $80,000 their loan would be roughly the same amount. The other big plus is that they can stop renting earlier and put the money towards their mortgage.

The case for waiting to save the full 20%

But what happens if this same property goes down in value by 15% over the next five years? Things don't look as good. Let's say, for example, that their home falls from $800,000 to $680,000 between 2020 and 2025.

TABLE 2 **WAITING AND AVOIDING LMI**

	2020 (10% DEPOSIT)	2025 (20% DEPOSIT)
Purchase price	$800,000	$680,000
Deposit required	$80,000	$136,000
LMI	$17,712	-
Loan amount	$737,712	$544,000

If Michael and David had waited, they would have avoided a loss in equity of $120,000 and they wouldn't have had to spend the extra $17,712 for LMI.

Their loan amount would have also been a lot less at $544,000 as opposed to $737,712 in 2020. And they'd have to save $24,000 less than they had anticipated to get a 20% deposit.

Of course, this is a very simple example. It does show, however, that if you buy well, when it comes to the property market, time is money and your biggest cost could be delaying your decision.

AM I BETTER OFF USING A SCHOLARSHIP FUND OR ETFs FOR MY KIDS' EDUCATION?

Chapter twenty

As every parent knows (or soon finds out), putting kids through 13 years of school involves a relentless pattern of dipping into your pocket. No matter whether you opt for the local public school or an elite private school, the same pattern applies of regularly forking out for everything from fees and uniforms, to sports gear, camps and excursions and, of course, the modern must-haves – a tablet or laptop computer.

If you've ever wondered about the final tally, research by Australian Scholarships Group (ASG, now Futurity Investment Group) found that from kindergarten to the end of year 12, the cost of educating your child can add up to:

- $68,727 in the public school system

- $127,027 in the Catholic system, or

- $298,689 in the independent school system.

The best way to navigate these costs is to plan ahead. One option is to grow a pool of cash savings. However, the low returns on cash mean you would have to tuck away ever-increasing amounts to meet the costs, which typically rise through secondary school and peak during years 11 and 12.

Another option is to make extra payments into your home loan or linked offset account. This way your money would at least earn a risk-free return equivalent to your mortgage interest rate – and potentially a higher after-tax return depending on your personal tax rate. Then, when a school bill needs to be paid you can just dip into the offset account or redraw the cash. The downside is that each time you withdraw money, you lose part of the interest savings that extra repayments or an offset account can provide. And, frankly, in today's low-interest environment, you could potentially earn higher returns on your spare cash by putting the money in other investments such as share-based ETFs.

A third option is to set up a separate investment dedicated to funding your child's education. Plenty of parents are interested in this strategy, and I'm often asked about 'scholarship plans' offered by ASG. In 2019, ASG rebranded to Futurity Investment Group, which now offers education bonds that work in a similar way. Let's take a closer look.

Education bonds

Education bonds are a type of managed investment that offer a tax-friendly way to save for schooling. Income earned on the bond's underlying investments is taxed at 30%, with tax paid by the bond issuer over the life of the bond if it is held for at least 10 years.

When money is drawn down to pay for school costs, the fund can claim the 30% tax back, a saving that's passed onto parents. After the 10-year period, earnings can be returned to investors 'tax-paid'. That's a plus for mums and dads whose marginal tax rate is above 30%. Bear in mind, if your annual income exceeds $37,001, you could be paying a marginal tax rate of 32.5%. So, you don't have to be a high-income earner to benefit.

After setting up your bond, you can keep adding to your investment through ongoing contributions as long as they meet the quirky 125% rule that is a feature of these bonds. This rule limits your annual contributions to no more than 125% of the previous year's investment. So, if you start out investing a total of $5,000 in year 1, the most you can contribute in year 2 is $6,250, and so on.

The 125% can have serious consequences. If you invest more than 125% of the prior year's contributions, the bond's 10-year tax period can reset, meaning it could take longer to get out your money tax-paid – and it's usually up to you to keep track of annual contributions.

What's interesting about education bonds is that your money is typically invested across a range of underlying managed funds that each charge fees of their own – a cost that is passed on to bond holders. In some cases, you can pay annual fees of around 1.25% on education bonds. This begs the question, could you do better yourself by investing directly in exchange traded funds (ETFs), which charge an average of 0.49% in annual fees? This is exactly what I'll look at next.

It's a close race

School fees are notorious for outstripping inflation, so as long as you start saving early it makes sense for any investment pitched at education costs to have exposure to growth assets such as shares. This is especially noteworthy if you choose an education bond. The bond issuer is likely to offer a range of investment choices for your bond – from 'conservative' to 'high growth'. The option you select will impact the returns your money earns. A conservative strategy, for example, may sound sensible but it will mean earning lower long-term returns.

Given that in 2020 private school fees rose by 2.83%, well above the rate of inflation of 1.8% at the start of the year, I have opted to compare a growth-focused education bond with a portfolio of ETFs, focusing on Australian shares.

It's worth noting that the figures in Table 1 on page 212 assume share-based ETFs generating an annual return averaging 6.5%. By contrast, even a 'growth focused' education bond can have up to 30% of the underlying investments in cash and fixed interest. This makes sense from the bond issuer's perspective as it needs to make allowance for parents withdrawing funds to pay for education costs. But it can mean the returns are slightly lower and, this being the case, I have allowed for annual returns averaging 6.0%.

Assuming an initial starting investment of $1,000, Table 1, shows how much you'd need to save each month to meet the projected school costs I mentioned earlier.

To cover the costs of a public school education, you'd need to invest around $280 each month with a growth-focused education bond, or $268 with ETFs. That's a difference of $12 per month.

If you have the Catholic school system in mind, you'd need to invest about $535 each month in the same education bond or $514 in your basket of ETFs – again a minor difference of $21 per month.

For an independent school, the required monthly investment ranges from $1,284 with an education bond through to $1,238 with ETFs – a difference of $46.

TABLE 1 **MONTHLY INVESTMENT REQUIRED TO COVER COSTS FROM K-12**

INVESTMENT OPTION[1]	PUBLIC SYSTEM TOTAL COST $68,727[2]	CATHOLIC SYSTEM TOTAL COST $127,027[2]	INDEPENDENT SYSTEM TOTAL COST $298,689[2]
Education Bond[3]	$280	$535	$1,284
Exchange Traded Funds[4]	$268	$514	$1,238

Source: aptwealth.com.au [1]Assumes savings start at $1,000 and rise by CPI (2.15%) annually over a 17-year period. [2]Total education costs for a child born in 2020, commencing kindergarten in 2025 and completing year 12 in 2038. [3]Assumes earnings of 6.0%pa and MER of 1.25%. [4]Assumed to focus on Australian shares, with 6.50%pa earnings and MER of 0.49%. Based on household income of Australian average of $116,584 with the investment held in the name of a non-income earner. Table provides indicative figures only and should not be regarded as applying to all families or taken as financial advice.

What to weigh up

Based on the figures in Table 1, it would appear that there's not much difference between education bonds and a portfolio of ETFs, but it's not that simple. There are other issues to weigh up.

TAX SAVINGS While education bonds can deliver attractive tax savings, share-based ETFs can also be very tax-friendly. The franking credits on underlying shares can be passed directly on to unitholders, and as long as you hold the ETF for more than 12 months, any profits on sale can attract a 50% capital gains tax discount.

COSTS TO GROW YOUR INVESTMENT A point in favour of education bonds is that it can cost nothing to grow your investment. You may pay zero fees to set up or add to an education bond.

That's not the case when you buy into (or sell) ETFs. If you're adding to an ETF portfolio on a monthly basis (as assumed in Table 1), even very cheap brokerage of $15 per trade can see the annual cost rise to $180.

THE EFFORT INVOLVED It's also worth thinking about how you'll manage your investment. Raising kids takes time and involvement, and from a practical perspective an education bond can be easy to live with. You invest the money and the bond issuer takes care of the rest.

ETFs can call for decisions around what to invest in and when. On top of this is the need to manage the paper trail of your portfolio for tax purposes.

FLEXIBILITY ETFs have a major point in their favour: the freedom to withdraw money for purposes unrelated to education expenses.

Depending on the education bond you buy into, you may – or may not – be able to withdraw money for purposes other than education. Even if you are able to do this, the tax treatment of your withdrawal can be complex, often depending on how long you've held the bond. With ETFs, you are free to use the money for whatever purpose you like, no questions asked.

Know what you're buying into

If you opt for education bonds, I stress the need to read the product disclosure statement thoroughly. These can be complex investments, and while there may be tax savings, there can also be tax consequences if you get it wrong. So, please be very sure about what you are buying into.

If you prefer to take a hands-on approach and you want flexibility around accessing your money, ETFs can tick plenty of boxes. They charge low fees, offer easy diversification and let you select investments based on your views of different asset markets.

If you're unsure about the investment strategy that is right for you and your family, it's not a bad idea to speak with a financial advisor.

SHOULD I PAY OFF MY MORTGAGE OR INVEST?

Chapter twenty-one

Should I pay off my mortgage or invest? If I'd received $1 from every person who's asked me that question over the past 20-odd years, I'd have at least an extra thousand dollars to put into my mortgage. Or, hang on, should I have added it to my super?

From a purely mathematical point of view, when interest rates are low, as they are now, you would probably get a better return on your money by investing it. If mortgage rates were higher, the answer could be different.

Let me explain. By paying off your mortgage, your return is equal to the rate on your loan – and it is tax-free. So, let's say you are paying 3.5%pa interest on your home loan then that is your 'guaranteed rate of return'.

Chances are you can get a better long-term return than that. To give you an idea, according to Vanguard, Australian shares returned 7.9%pa on average over the 10 years to 31 December 2019. International shares returned 12.3%pa over the same period and Australian property grew by 11.5%pa on average. Looking at super funds, the median balanced accumulation option returned 7.7%pa over the decade to the end of 2019, according to SuperRatings.

It's important to remember, though, that investing will mean you are taking on higher risk than you would by simply popping your extra cash onto your mortgage. You also have to factor in tax, which can reduce that return.

Put simply, if the investment returns are 8% and your marginal tax rate is 34.5% (including the Medicare Levy), your after-tax return will be 5.24%. That is still higher than mortgage rates at the moment. This doesn't apply to superannuation because investment earnings generated by your super are taxed at a maximum rate of 15%.

Now if the rate on your home loan was closer to 5%, ploughing any extra cash into your mortgage might be a safer bet. That rate of return is essentially guaranteed, unlike with investments in riskier asset classes, and you'll probably sleep better at night.

Let's take a look at a hypothetical example of how the numbers stack up if you're deciding between, say, your mortgage and super. Chloe, 35, has a spare $200 a month. As the table below shows, if she used it to top up her super, she would have $73,688 more in super when she turns 60 than she would if she had relied on just the super guarantee.

TABLE 1 **SUPERANNUATION RETIREMENT BALANCE PROJECTION – EXTRA ONGOING AFTER-TAX CONTRIBUTION**

	BASE SCENARIO	**EXTRA $200 PER MONTH**
Starting age	35	35
Average gross annual income	$86,237	$86,237
Average starting balance	$51,740	$51,740
Average annual investment returns	7.30%	7.30%
Account balance at age 60 (today's dollars)	$374,125	$477,814
Difference to base scenario at age 60	-	$73,688

Source: www.canstar.com.au, 14/07/20. Based on a 35-year-old with a starting balance of $51,740, starting gross annual income of $86,237. SG contribution amounts per government announced rates. Total extra contributions over 25 years equal a total amount of $60,000. Investment returns assumed to be 7.30%pa. Net performance deducts average fees of 1.11%pa. Average life insurance premium of $189 (increasing with inflation each year) is assumed charged at the end of each year based on products in Canstar's database for an average balance of $80k and age of 45. Account balance is displayed in 'today's dollars', meaning the value is adjusted for inflation. Please note all information on income, annual superannuation fees and performance returns are used for illustrative purposes only. Actual returns and the value of your investment may fall as well as rise from year to year; this example does not take such variation into account.

If Chloe added that $200 to her mortgage instead, she would have improved her situation by $58,172 (equity includes interest savings). So, based on these numbers, topping up her super gives Chloe a better result. It's important to note that all the figures are in today's dollars.

Keep in mind the numbers will vary based on your individual situation including your age, salary, marginal tax rate, super balance, size of your mortgage and interest rates.

Even though the numbers may tell you that you'd be better off investing, it doesn't mean that's the path you have to take. There are a number of things to consider when weighing up your options. These include things such as how much of your mortgage you have paid off, interest rates, tax and when you want to access your money.

TABLE 2 **IMPACT OF EXTRA $200 CONTRIBUTED TO MONTHLY MORTGAGE REPAYMENT**

	BASE SCENARIO	EXTRA $200 PER MONTH
Starting age	35	35
Starting property price	$500,000	$500,000
Annual property price growth	3.67%	3.67%
Interest rate	4.41%	4.41%
Equity at age 60 (today's dollars)	$605,788	$663,960
Difference in equity		$58,172

Source: www.canstar.com.au, 14/07/20. Total extra contributions over 25 years equals a total amount of $60,000. Average annual property price growth based on annualised property price percentage change over the past five years using ABS Residential Property Price Indexes, March 2020. Interest rate based on average variable, principal and interest, owner occupier loans in Canstar's database, taken over the past five years to march 2020. Equity at age 60 is displayed in 'today's dollars', meaning the value is adjusted for inflation.

HOW MUCH OF YOUR MORTGAGE YOU HAVE PAID OFF ALREADY

If your mortgage is 'fresh', it can make sense to focus on that first. That's because when you first take out a loan, interest accounts for a larger proportion of your repayment than principal so the more you pay off earlier, the less interest you'll pay over the long term.

A general rule of thumb is that you should have 50% equity in the family home before you start investing any extra money in other assets.

THE AMOUNT YOU HAVE IN SAVINGS

It's important to have some sort of cash buffer before you start investing. You want to have a stash of cash readily available in case of an emergency. You may want to have at least six months' worth of expenses set aside before investing.

HOW MUCH TAX YOU'LL NEED TO PAY

When you are looking at the potential returns of investments you should factor in the amount of tax you need to pay on any investment income. You may also have to pay capital gains tax if you sell the investment for a profit. If you have held the investment for more than 12 months though you'll get a 50% discount.

On the flipside, there may be tax perks on some investments such as fully-franked shares or super. Any before-tax money that you put into super is taxed at just 15% (as opposed to whatever your marginal tax rate is). You may also be able to claim a tax deduction if you make an after-tax contribution. It pays to get expert tax advice.

INTEREST RATES

This comes down to what I wrote about earlier. What rate are you paying on your mortgage and do you think you could get a higher rate of return if you invest elsewhere? When rates are low there is a good chance you can get a higher return by investing.

WHAT MAKES YOU MOST COMFORTABLE

You might prefer to buy your own home before you start building wealth in other asset classes. The sense of security you get from owning your own home might be more important to you, so it's a matter of personal preference.

WHEN YOU WANT ACCESS TO YOUR MONEY

If you think you'll want access to your money in the next couple of years then it might be better to pay off your mortgage and have the money available through redraw or offset. So, it's still helping to reduce the interest on your home loan but it's fairly easy to get your hands on if you need it for school fees, a holiday or renovations, for instance.

If you have the money invested in shares or an ETF you may still be able to access it, but if you need it in a hurry and markets are down you may end up having to lock in any losses.

And, of course, you'll have an even longer wait if you want to take money out of your super. You need to meet a 'condition of release', such as reaching your preservation age and retiring; or reaching your preservation age and choosing to begin a transition to retirement income stream while you are still working or are 65 years old (even if you have not retired). You also never know when the rules around super may change, so this could be different in the future.

You may also be able to get early access to super on compassionate grounds if you're in financial hardship but there are a lot of hoops you'll have to jump through.

Personally, I am a fan of doing a combination of both – putting that little bit extra towards the mortgage but also directing some of your spare cash to build up wealth outside the family home. It's best to get independent financial advice to figure out what may work better for you.

SHOULD I HAVE AN SMSF?

Chapter twenty-two

This is something I have asked myself from time to time – should I have a self-managed super fund (SMSF)? But when I have pondered this question, I have come to the same conclusion: for me it's a no. The main reason is time – or rather lack of it. You need to have a fair bit of spare time to manage your own super and at this stage in my life, I really don't think I have enough time to do it properly. Another reason is that I invest outside of super so I'm happy to leave my super to be managed by the professionals.

That's just me. Obviously, many others feel differently. Australian Taxation Office (ATO) figures show that there were 581,231 SMSFs with a total of 1,090,467 members as at June 2019. Interestingly, though, while 20,427 were established in the year to June 2019, 13,544 were wound up over the same period.

If you are thinking about setting up an SMSF, first weigh up the pros and cons. Here are some factors to consider.

The returns

This is definitely a key factor. You need to be fairly confident that you can make the right investment decisions and that they will produce a better result than what you'd get from a retail or industry fund.

As you can see from the chart on the next page, APRA-regulated funds had a better average return in three out of the five periods considered. ATO statistics show that funds with larger balances tend to achieve a better return. For example, in 2017-2018, funds with a balance of between $50,000 and $100,000 returned -4.7%pa on average while funds with between $1 million and $2 million in assets returned 8.4%.

AVERAGE RETURNS FOR SMSFs AND APRA-REGULATED FUNDS

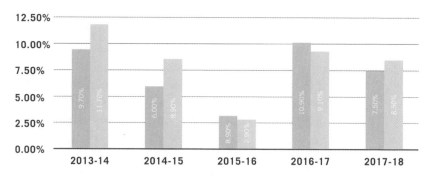

Source: ATO. Self-managed super funds: a statistical overview 2017–18.

YOUR SUPER BALANCE

How much money do you have in super? Now it's worth noting that you can have up to four members in an SMSF, so think about who will be part of the fund and how much combined super you have.

There is always some debate about how much you should have but most experts suggest at least $500,000. You may be happy to start with a smaller balance if you think it will reach $500,000 in the next few years.

YOUR TIME

You can't just set and forget your SMSF. You will need to spend some time each month not only choosing your investments but managing paperwork and making sure you stick to the rules. How much time?

According to the Investment Trends, SMSF Investor Report, from March 2018, trustees have spent about 8.4 hours a month, on average, managing their SMSF. That is effectively more than 100 hours over the year.

THE COSTS

You'll need to factor in set-up fees as well as ongoing expenses. The cost to set up an SMSF will vary based on whether there are individual trustees or corporate trustees. The fees range anywhere from about $500 to $2,000. In the 2018 financial year, the average operating cost was $6,152 and the median was $3,923. Other expenses that may come with running an SMSF include interest expenses, insurance premiums and investment expenses.

THE RULES

There are a lot of rules and if you break any of them you can end up with a fine. Even if you get professional help, you are the one responsible for making sure you are complying with the law.

One of the main rules is that all investments need to pass the 'sole purpose test'. According to the ATO, this means your fund needs to be maintained for the sole purpose of providing retirement benefits to your members, or to their dependants, if a member dies before retirement.

INVESTING IN PROPERTY THROUGH AN SMSF

One of the reasons people like the idea of having an SMSF is that they can use it to invest in property. There are tax benefits associated with owning a property as part of your SMSF. Rental income earned by the property is taxed at a concessional rate of 15% and the capital gain will also be taxed at a discounted rate.

If you're borrowing money to fund the purchase, it needs to be done under a 'limited recourse borrowing arrangement'. There are pretty strict conditions and it can take longer to get approved than a standard loan and rates tend to be higher. It's also important that the fund has enough cashflow to be able to make the repayments on the loan.

There are quite a few rules you will need to follow. For example, property must have been included as part of your investment strategy, you can't live in the home yourself and it can't be lived in or rented by a member, their family or associates. Commercial property is different and you may be able to rent that to anyone (even to yourself or another fund member) as long as they are paying market rate and meet certain conditions.

Investing in property through your SMSF can be quite complex and what I have included here is just the tip of the iceberg.

There's no straight yes or no answer here. It's worth getting some expert advice, preferably from somebody who specialises in SMSFs.

Acknowledgements

Dear Editor,

Had it not been for your hundreds of emails (often sent in the middle of the night), constant phone calls and messages, a demanding schedule and an absurd to-do list, this book would have been written in half the time.

Having said that, though, it would only be half as good. Thank you, my dear friend Maria Bekiaris, for once again agreeing to take on the role of editor of my book. It's always easier to work with someone who shares the same values ... 'education and empowerment' has been our mantra and it's wonderful to be able to put our knowledge and excitement about what we do onto these pages.

A big thank you also to Nicola Field who once again led the research on this book. There is no mucking around with this lady. Nicola, I thank you for making sure I got the facts right and kept the strategies real.

It was also a pleasure to be able to once again call on the expertise of behavioural economist and author *Going Ape S#!t!*, Phil Slade, for the Mastering Your Money Mindset section. I've long understood that there's more to money than dollars and cents and your insights into our financial attitudes and monetary behaviours were invaluable.

Finally, a standing ovation for the production team ... David Scotto, Jeannel Cunanan and Stephanie Kistner for making this book sing, and for allowing me to bring in my trusted glam team – David Connelly, Eloise Proust and Alex Wilson. I know you should never judge a book by its cover but clearly my production team thought it was best not to shoot me as if I had just rolled out of bed – it's amazing what a box of products can do!

Feel free now to rest your coffee cup on my face, but I'm hoping that you can't put the book down long enough for it to leave a coffee stain.